MARDUKITE MASTER COURSE
ACADEMY LECTURES
VOL. 2

DRUIDS,
ELVES & DRAGONS

Titles in this series by Joshua Free:
Vol.1 – Magick & Mysticism
Vol.2 – Druids, Elves & Dragons
Vol.3 – Mesopotamian Tradition
Vol.4 – Mardukite Systemology

Mardukite Research Library Catlogue No. "MMC-1D"

Based on the Lectures by Joshua Free for the
Mardukite Master Course given during September 2020
excerpted from *The Complete Mardukite Master Course*

Every effort has been given to match wording and inflection for lecture transcripts based on the recordings made by Mardukite Academy of Systemology

Published from
Mardukite Borsippa HQ, San Luis Valley, Colorado

cum superiorum privilegio veniaque

The Founding Church of Mardukite Zuism,
Mardukite Academy & Systemology Society

MARDUKITE ACADEMY – COLLECTOR'S EDITION

MARDUKITE MASTER COURSE ACADEMY LECTURES VOL. 2

DRUIDS, ELVES & DRAGONS

Based on the Lectures
by Joshua Free

THE JOSHUA FREE IMPRINT
JFI PUBLICATIONS

© 2022, JOSHUA FREE

ISBN : 979-8-986-43790-3

No part of this publication may be reproduced in any form or by any means, electronic or mechanical, including photocopying, recording, or any information storage or retrieval system, without permission from the publisher. This book is not intended to substitute medical treatment or professional advice.

*The Mardukite Academy Lectures
given during September 2020
for Academy Grade-I Route-D of the
Mardukite Master Course regarding
Druids & The Dragon Tradition.*

Mardukite Academy Collector's Edition — *July 2022*
mardukite.com

The _Original_ Master Course Lectures

Commemorating his silver anniversary and drawing from 25 years of experiential esoteric research and underground literary developments, world-renowned mystic philosopher and prodigious occult author, Joshua Free, provides the professional qualifications necessary for "mastering" upper-level understanding of his collected works in the same way that an artist "masters" their craft. Nothing is held back in this surprisingly candid presentation of materials.

This is volume two of a four-part series, providing a serious Seeker with full transcripts to 12 of the 48 Academy Lectures previously published in the mega-anthology "Complete Mardukite Master Course."

Here you will find an insightful tome demonstrating a refreshing approach to understanding Druids, the Dragon Legacy and Elven-Faerie in the 21st century.

Although recent years have seen an advancement in the work, all publications by Joshua Free, written and published between 1995 and 2019, pertain to a singular continuum of complete instruction divided into three knowledge tiers or "Grades." A complete library collection of all "core material" described in the "Mardukite Master Course" was also reissued in four different Master Edition textbooks: "The Great Magickal Arcanum," "Merlyn's Complete Book of Druidism," "Necronomicon: The Complete Anunnaki Legacy" and "The Systemology Handbook" – totaling 3,600 pages in all.

Now YOU can experience the legendary "Master Course" from anywhere in the Universe, exactly as given in-person by Joshua Free to the "Mardukite Academy of Systemology" in September 2020.

THE GRADE-I ROUTE-D ACADEMY LECTURES

INTRODUCTIONS

Introducing the Mardukite Master Course . . . 9

Materials of the Mardukite Master Course . . . 17

Mardukite Master Course Training Schedule . . . 19

Introducing Grade-I Route-D Materials . . . 21

THE ACADEMY LECTURES (GRADE-I ROUTE-D)

1—13. The Druid School (*Sept. 23, 2020*) . . . 24

2—14. Druid Fundamentals (*Sept. 23, 2020*) . . . 37

3—15. Druid Philosophy (*Sept. 23, 2020*) . . . 50

4—16. Druid Ritual Tech (*Sept. 23, 2020*) . . . 64

5—17. The Elvenomicon (*Sept. 23, 2020*) . . . 78

6—18. Danubian Druidism (*Sept. 23, 2020*) . . . 91

7—19. Faerie Traditions (*Sept. 23, 2020*) . . . 104

8—20. Otherworld Tech (*Sept. 23, 2020*) . . . 118

9—21. Natural Paths (*Sept. 24, 2020*) . . . 131

10—22. Ogham Tech (*Sept. 24, 2020*) . . . 145

11—23. The Draconomicon (*Sept. 24, 2020*) . . . 160

12—24. Grade-I Review Session (*Sept. 24, 2020*) . . . 174

APPENDIX

Suggested Reading and Additional Materials . . . 189

INTRODUCING THE MARDUKITE MASTER COURSE

The single most purpose of our *Mardukite Master Course* is to ensure, certify and provide professional qualifications for "mastering" an understanding of the materials in the same way that an artist "masters" their craft. The complete *Mardukite Master Course* spans three *Grades* of knowledge and is given only to those *Seekers* that first properly worked through all three *Grades*, and may then be rightfully considered *Masters* of this knowledge. Extents of such "mastery" should prove readily obvious (objectively), lending to increased qualities of *Self-Actualization*, personal leadership and the certainty to manage and instruct *Mardukite Groups*.

Current works available by Joshua Free—written and published between 1995 and 2019—all pertain to a singular stream of complete instruction that is divided into three *Grades* or knowledge tiers. The *Mardukite Master Course* is intended to grant a clear unification of material presented across all three *Grades* under the banner of "Mardukite Systemology," which is also the name given to *Grade-III*. The two are interconnected (*Grade-III* and the *Master Course*); hence the complete *Mardukite Master Course* is only delivered to *Seekers* at the completion of *Grade-III*. There are "higher" *Grades* within the domain of "NexGen Systemology," but the *Mardukite Master Course* successfully covers all specifically "Mardukite Master" *Grades*: I, II and III.

It is important to clarify what we mean by *Grades* and distinguish the materials that pertain to each. In most instances, instruction for these *Grades*—as delivered in the materials (books) over the past 25 years—was all self-administered; meaning it has been explored independent of properly structured groups or trained instructors. In the past, *Seekers* selected a volume at random, had at it on their own for a while, then walked away with whatever level of understanding might be attained, even if severely fragmented. Most are unaware that the works—no matter the theme—are all tied together. They are divided as follows:

GRADE-I	Western Magical Tradition ("Magick")
GRADE-II	Ancient Mystery School of Mesopotamia
GRADE-III	Futurist/NexGen Mardukite Systemology

It can be said that the *Grades* are all a part of a single continuum—one which is explored in a "reverse engineering" style in order to provide the greatest certainty for effective workable future applications that will advance the spiritual evolution of the *Human Condition*, particularly the *Self* that is participating in and experiencing a co-creation of the Physical Universe and a continued existence of its conditions. As a single continuum, the *Grades* do actually overlap on many points—and often times these "bridges" between levels of understanding are what we are highlighting profusely for our *Mardukite Master Course*. This preferred approach—treating the universal knowledge and its records as a single wholeness rather than an emphasis on individual parts—developed after many years of experiment and discovery.

Direction of the *Mardukite Master Course* loosely follows a chronological pathway charted by Joshua Free from 1995 through 2019—meaning: from the release of the first "Merlyn Stone" *Grade-I* discourses on "magick" and "Druidism" until the recent completion of *Grade-III* as "Mardukite Systemology." Between these *Grades*, a *Seeker* discovers abundant source material known as the "Mardukite Core" comprising *Grade-II*. These *Grades* also loosely follow a premise for organization set out in the 1990's for *Grade-I* Alumni of "Merlyn Stone's School of Magick"[*] that is referred to elsewhere as "The Sacred Order of the Crystal Dawn." The outline for this premise in 1999 proposed the structuring of "A New Illuminati" using the work published by Joshua Free over the next two decades.

---

[*] Also operating 1998-2000 as "The Elven Fellowship Circle of Magick" in Denver.

There are no strictly enforced "title-badges" and/or "initiations" defining *Grades* when applied to individual *Mardukite Groups* (outside the religious organizational function of *Mardukite Zuism* specifically) for "study" or "instructive" purposes. A *Master* may choose to adopt a particular regimen for their *Seekers* as applicable to each *Grade* and in alignment with the theme and goals of the group. Starting with the original *Grade-I* "Merlyn Stone" volume by Joshua Free—THE SORCERER'S HANDBOOK—reissued for its 21st Anniversary as a collector's edition hardcover, sufficient material is now available in each "core" toward defining group structure as it pertains to the greater "*whole*" at each *Grade*.

Parameters assigned to formal progressive *Grades* are approximately equivalent to the *first three* "*degrees*" of the "Crystal Dawn" program; which is the extent an individual "Chapter" or "Lodge" is allowed to administer (apart from authority of a "Grand Lodge"). For two decades, this clause permitted a *Master* of the *Third Degree* to launch a "Chapter" or "Group" as an official extension of the organization; so long as the *Seeker* had completed the *Master Course*. However, no such *Grade-III* materials were sufficiently supplied as a "core" until 2019 to make this possible.

The basic pattern of development across the *Grades* follows progressive and cumulative ascent up the "Ladder of Lights" or "Gateways to Infinity" first described by the Ancient Mystery School of Mesopotamia as a sevenfold "Babylonian Stargate" system. The chronology of the *Grades* begins with the most apparent and recent influences of the contemporary "New Age"; meaning the modern communication and conception of "magick" and metaphysics—otherwise known as the Western Magical Tradition, which maintained its popularity for the past several thousand years in Europe. This is the essence of *Grade-I*, which is essentially the "*Lunar Gate*."

A *Seeker* exploring origins behind magickal correspondences, practices, ceremonies and ritualism of various European developments—including everything from ancient Celtic Druids to more modern esoteric Hermetic Orders—will at one juncture or another intersect with the even older Ancient Mystery School present in Mesopotamia—systematized in "Mardukite Babylon" at the inception of the *Age of Aries* (c. 2160 B.C.)—an extension of the former loosely organized Sumerian civilization, now collectively making up *Grade-II* and the key to open the "*Nabu Gate*."

When a *Seeker* considers this logical progression: we begin with what is most readily familiar and accessible at *Grade-I*, loading the shot in the sling, and then pulling back to the extent that we may be certain, by examining the oldest literary records in *Grade-II*; the very basis for which our *Grade-I* material is actually based, albeit forgotten to the sands of time coupled with thousands of years of programming and encoding separating the two. History and tradition begins with "writing," and so we cannot be certain of anything further than what we have actual accounts of; yet still we find that these *Arcane Tablets* provide an understanding that is milestones beyond what is demonstrated in contemporary society today.

There are many ways of which we can demonstrate how the knowledge between these two *Grades* is bridged and overlaps in application and study; but the *Grades* are distinguished as they are for good reason—and we are not to muddy the waters of a *Seeker's* thinking by incorporating unnecessary complications to instruction. A line has been drawn, if only even from necessity, between the *Grades* by using the *Mardukite Chamberlains Grade-II* material as a benchmark for our evaluation of other materials.

Essentially—all volumes by Joshua Free pertaining exclusively to ancient Mesopotamia are considered *Grade-II*; all volumes pertaining to general mysticism, magick, esoterica, Druidism, &tc are considered *Grade-I*. This is not to say that "higher realizations" are inaccessible from lower *Grade* materials, nor is there a guarantee that "higher realizations" are gleaned directly from reading higher *Grade* materials. A *Seeker* working through the entirety of the first two *Grades* may reach all necessary "ledges" of "knowing" on their own merit, independent of outside instruction. But given that only one-way communication relay takes place from this book-learning, there is no guarantee that an individual will correctly gauge the distance between "ledges" of "knowing" on their ascent up as they leap about unaided.

An early premise of "higher" *Grades* comprised an ORIGINAL THESIS for a new flavor of "New Thought" provided exclusively to *Grade-II* Mardukite Alumni in 2011 as "NexGen Systemology." The official "Core" of *Grade-III* was not released to the public by Joshua Free until late 2019 as "Mardukite Systemology." It is from the vantage point of *Grade-III*, and a mastery of that same tier of knowledge, that we actually treat all of which the *Mardukite Master Course* represents. Although a *Seeker* could certainly remain at one or another *Grade*, an individual must demonstrate total understanding of all three *Grades* to be officially considered a *Master*.

Earliest contributions toward this *Course* from the 1990's are considered *Grade-I*, pertaining to practical magick, general metaphysics, the Western Magical Tradition and its archetypal scions, the *Druids*. The original *Grade-I* volumes pertaining to magick and metaphysics are THE SORCERER'S HANDBOOK and ARCANUM by Joshua Free. In addition to THE DRUID'S HANDBOOK, there are two volumes that both complete the *Druid Cycle* and effectively "bridge" to *Grade-II* elements that incorporate Mesopotamia: DRACONOMICON and ELVENOMICON.[*]

A *Seeker* working through the original *Grade-I* "Handbooks" may also choose to take an alternate "bridge" between the ritualism and ceremonialism of *Grade-I* with *Grade-II*, as des-

---

[*] *"Elvenomicon"* formerly released as *"Book of Elven-Faerie"* (from 2004 to 2018) by Joshua Free.

cribed in THE VAMPYRE'S HANDBOOK by Joshua Free.* The original 2015 release of these materials for *Moroii ad Vitam Paramus* served as a contemporary "holding point" for Alumni after the completion of *Grade-II* work, while a "Core" for *Grade-III* developed behind-the-scenes until late 2019. For our purposes, this now means that there are several "entry" points for a *Seeker* to experience glamour and enchantment of the *Grade-I* "*Lunar Gate*" on the way to higher avenues of *Self-Actualization*—which is the ultimate goal behind the *Master* level.

In 2008, existing ARCANUM and ELVENOMICON materials contributed to the establishment of *Mardukite Ministries*, an underground umbrella organization that took control of the former "Merlyn Stone" legacy of Joshua Free as a "ledge" for developing *Grade-II*. By 2009, the *Mardukite Chamberlains* emerged—a global network contributing to progressive generation and dissemination of a "Mardukite Core" of materials, providing the inception of the modern "Mardukite" (and "Mardukite Zuism") paradigms. This living spiritual philosophy dispensed at *Grade-II* is drawn heavily from the ancient cuneiform tablet records of Mesopotamia/Babylon.

Mardukite Chamberlains participated in developing the bulk of material for *Grade-II* from 2009 through 2011. These materials were simultaneously presented in two guises—the *same* materials, but dispensed in two different formats: one emphasizing the *Anunnaki Legacy* as a demonstration of more "academic" and "intellectual" pursuits into ancient history and its esoteric traditions; the other, emphasizing the title of the NECRONOMICON due to the high correlation and association of "New Age" data regarding the ancient "Mardukite Babylonian" tradition. When treated in its entirety as the *Complete Anunnaki Legacy* from within the Mardukite paradigm, presentation of the two "formats" is essentially identical. *Grade-II* should not, however, be confu-

---

* *"The Vampyre's Handbook"* formerly released as *"Vampyre Magick"* by Joshua Free; an anthology edition containing *"Vampyre Bible"* and *"Cybernomicon."*

sed with *any* other outside treatment of the "*Necronomicon*" subject.

Starting in 2009, the original source book of *Grade-II* developed into an anthology composed from individual discourses produced for the *Mardukite Chamberlains* and compiled into NECRONOMICON: THE ANUNNAKI BIBLE. Then, over the next two years, several key elements were added to expand the source book; additionally, several volumes were added to the *Grade-II* core, including Joshua Free's GATES OF THE NECRONOMICON and NECRONOMICON: THE ANUNNAKI GRIMOIRE.[‡] These anthologies contain several stand-alone discourses in themselves—all of which were consolidated into a complete *Grade-II* mega-anthology titled NECRONOMICON: THE COMPLETE ANUNNAKI LEGACY (with a special *10th Anniversary Master Edition* released in early 2020).

The gradation (*Grades*) structure and concept of the *Mardukite Master Course* was announced in August 2019 at THE TABLETS OF DESTINY lectures, as described (from transcripts) in the *Grade-III* text of the same title:—

> "Some of you that have been really following along through the materials over the years already have an understanding, from the *Grades* previously provided... And this is one of the keys or secrets held by the *Master*—an individual who has a complete workable understanding of these various levels and degrees represented in former instruction, but they are not themselves formally attached to any of it—drawing up only those solid examples suitable for citation, example and demonstration. So, that's what a Master is, and we are referring now to this intermediary *Grade-III* 'Mardukite Systemology' material as the *Master*

[‡] *"Gates of the Necronomicon"* anthology includes *"The Sumerian Legacy"* and *"Necronomicon Revelations -or- Crossing to the Abyss"*; *"Necronomicon Grimoire"* anthology includes "*The Complete Book of Marduk by Nabu*" and "*The Maqlu Ritual Book.*"

Grade. I expect to also develop a formal instruction course for that, which will solidify the unification of the extant 'Mardukite Core' and NexGen Systemology for this Grade."—*Joshua Free*

The other significant portion of *Grade-III* material is found within the textbook for the CRYSTAL CLEAR Mardukite Systemology Self-Defragmentation Course Program developed by Joshua Free and officially released in December 2019, so as to make certain that proper introductory tools were available for the 2020's decade to usher in a *NexGen* evolution in consciousness. *Grade-III* emphasizes strengthening personal certainty and management of "Reality," employing spiritual philosophies of "Mardukite Systemology." This is our launch point for all further upper-level *Grades*, just as much as it is a capstone representing minimum requirements for our *Mardukite Master Course*—intended to treat all material of *Grades I, II* and *III*.

MATERIALS OF THE
MARDUKITE MASTER COURSE

Since 2009, materials comprising the *Mardukite Research Library* have included all officially published works by Joshua Free to date. From 2008 through 2018, management and responsibility of these materials fell upon the *Mardukite Truth Seeker Press* governed by *Mardukite Ministries* and maintained by the *Mardukite Chamberlains*. As of 2018, a consistent transfer of official responsibility for all materials is increasingly assumed by the *Joshua Free Publishing Imprint*.

Throughout the years, a continuous development ensued, contributing to the release of many materials—including both those mentioned previously in this introduction, and other supplemental works that have appeared or are reissued for posterity. As the work progressed, goals for refinement and consolidation of the knowledge were repeatedly observed in newer editions and publications. Up until recently, the work was exceptionally "fluid" and required considerable attention over the course of its development. Information and discourses were released as they were discovered or refined for many years before appearing as the newly revised "collected works" anthologies and other "collector's editions" in the past year—making the materials more accessible and comprehensible than ever before possible. Goal attained.

It is of benefit for the *Seeker* (and *Master-in-Training*) to see an outright listing of all available graded materials (and their supplements) considered for inclusion as the *Mardukite Master Course*. Titles given represent the most current editions at the time of preparing this introduction. Some *Seekers* may already be in possession of former editions of these materials; and while the titles may change—and volumes may be collected for various anthologies—any *"Liber"*[*] designations used to catalogue the *Mardukite Resear*-

---

[*] The term *Liber* (meaning *book*) is used by esoteric organizations to

ch Library remain fixed to a particular discourse or release in perpetuity. This means, regardless of whatever "title" may be attached to, for example, *Liber-50* (or whatever anthology it may appear in), the material designated "*Liber-50*" is always *Liber-50*, in any of its formats or revisions. Although some *Seekers* have not taken note of these *liber designations*, this internal consistency has been maintained openly and publicly for over a decade.

---

title their work.

MARDUKITE MASTER COURSE TRAINING SCHEDULE

|| GRADE-I || ROUTE OF MAGICK & METAPHYSICS ||

Primary Textbooks:[∞]
        THE SORCERER'S HANDBOOK
        ARCANUM: GREAT MAGICAL ARACNUM
Supplementary:
Additional: *Route of Druidism & The Dragon Legacy*

|| GRADE-I || ROUTE OF DRUIDISM & THE DRAGON LEGACY ||

Primary Textbooks:[*]
        THE DRUID'S HANDBOOK (*Liber-D Series*)
        ELVENOMICON (*Liber-D Series*)
        DRACONOMICON (*Liber-D Series*)

Supplementary:
        THE VAMPYRE'S HANDBOOK
        --The Vampyre's Bible (*Liber V*)
        --Cybernomicon (*Liber V2*)
Optional: *Draconomicon Vol.2: The Pheryllt Researches*
Additional: *Route of Mesopotamian Mysteries*

|| GRADE-II || ROUTE OF MESOPOTAMIAN MYSTERIES ||

Primary Textbooks:[‡]
        NECRONOMICON: THE ANUNNAKI BIBLE
         (-or- THE COMPLETE ANUNNAKI BIBLE)
        --Mardukite Tablet Catalogue (*Liber-N,L,G,9*)
        --The Book of Sajaha-the-Seer (*Liber-S*)
        GATES OF THE NECRONOMICON
        --Sumerian Religion (*Liber-50*)
        --Babylonian Myth & Magic (*Liber-51+E*)

[∞] Grade-I, Route-A Anthology also available—*"The Great Magickal Arcanum"* (2020 Hardcover) by Joshua Free.

[*] Grade-I, Route-D Anthology also available—*"Merlyn's Complete Book of Druidism"* (Hardcover) by Joshua Free.

[‡] Grade-II Anthology also available—*"Necronomicon: The Complete Anunnaki Legacy"* (Hardcover) by Joshua Free.

--Necronomicon Revelations (*Liber-R*)
--Crossing to the Abyss (*Liber-555*)
NECRONOMICON: ANUNNAKI GRIMOIRE
  (-or- PRACTICAL BABYLONIAN MAGIC)
--Babylonian Magic (*Liber-E*)
--The Book of Marduk by Nabu (*Liber-W*)
--The Maqlu Ritual Book (*Liber-M*)
--Enochian Magician's Handbook (*Liber-K*)
Supplementary: Optnl: *The Anunnaki Tarot* (*Liber-T*)
              Addnl: *Route of Mardukite Systemology*

|| GRADE-III || ROUTE OF MARDUKITE SYSTEMOLOGY ||

Primary Textbooks:[∞]

      THE TABLETS OF DESTINY (*Liber-One*)
      CRYSTAL CLEAR (*Liber-2B*)

Supplementary:

      SYSTEMOLOGY: ORIGINAL THESIS (*Liber-S-1X*)
      THE POWER OF ZU (*Liber-S-1Z*)

Optional: *Pantheisticon (300th Anniversary Edition)*
Additional: *Route of The Mardukite Master Course*
            Route of Professional Piloting (Grade-IV+)

[∞] Grade-III Anthology also available—*"The Systemology Handbook"* (Hardcover) by Joshua Free.

INTRODUCING GRADE-I ROUTE-D MATERIALS

Greetings fellow Truth Seekers!

Welcome to the *Mardukite Master Course* for the *Grade-I "D-Cycle"* materials!

When first starting up the *Grade-I* work—which is the first steps plotted toward a higher knowingness of *Life, the Universe and Everything*—the *Mardukite Master Course* issues two potential routes; which are greatly complimentary and not especially exclusive to each other. The necessary materials for *Grade-I* may be acquired from the *Joshua Free Publishing Imprint* (formerly *Mardukite Truth Seeker Press*).

Our *Mardukite Master Course* for *Grade-I "Route of Druidism"* and/or "Mardukite Druidry" work starts, of course, with a lot of reading—the *"Liber-D Cycle"*—and, if you are so inclined, a significant amount of "energy play" and "mystical experiments"—all of which are intended to lead a *Seeker* to higher personal realizations.

But...where to begin?

There are three core units composing the "Route of Druidism"—each contained within one of the core textbooks of the *Liber-D Cycle* by Joshua Free: DRACONOMICON, THE DRUID'S HANDBOOK and ELVENOMICON (formerly known as *Book of Elven-Faerie*)—in addition to other published *Pheryllt Researches*. I list these here in the order they were released; not necessarily as a sequence of study.

Unlike *Grade-II*, where a *Seeker* may be unwaveringly directed to its original core source book—NECRONOMICON: THE ANUNNAKI BIBLE—as a most logical place to start, the *Grade-I* materials have not previously been so clearly structured; now even treated as two individual avenues: the *"Route of Magick & Metaphysics"* and the *"Route of Druidism & The Dragon Legacy."* The *Liber-D Cycle* materials pertain specifically to this second Route. The two Routes are not mutually exclusive and present two correlated approaches to the "Western Magical Tradition."

As of March 2020, the entire *Liber-D Cycle* and *Pheryllt Researches* also appear in a single Master Edition volume: MERLYN'S COMPLETE BOOK OF DRUIDISM.

The arrival of MERLYN'S COMPLETE BOOK OF DRUIDISM now puts an entire Esoteric Research Library of *Grade-I— Route of Druidism*, collected writings by Joshua Free spanning a quarter-of-a-century—since 1995—accessibly at a *Seeker's* fingertips in one single volume! In light of this, some *Seeker's* may find approaching a mighty tome like MERLYN'S COMPLETE BOOK OF DRUIDISM for their core instruction somewhat intimidating when not treated systematically.

Each volume of the "Druid Core" or "Druid Trilogy" by Joshua Free approaches the subject of Druidism from its own angle—and prior to the release of MERLYN'S COMPLETE BOOK OF DRUIDISM, its author had not fixed its sequence of study in place. This resolution is what makes the *Mardukite Master Course* for this material—and a coherent omnibus volume of the complete library—even possible.

The sequence of study for the *Grade-I "Route of Druidism"* is as follows:

1. THE DRUID'S HANDBOOK (*"Druidry"*)
2. ELVENOMICON (*"Book of Elven-Faerie"*)
3. THE DRACONOMICON

This same recommended sequence correlates to the arrangement of materials for MERLYN'S COMPLETE BOOK OF DRUIDISM—which is supplemented with a collection of *Pheryllt Researches*[*] as an "appendix" for the same volume. These additional *Pheryllt Researches* were not presented as

---

[*] Published in 2022 as *"Draconomicon Vol. 2: Pheryllt Researches."*

part of the original "Core." They may be studied as a supplement to the final volume: DRACONOMICON or else treated as an *extension course* of the original "Core" as a reinforcement to ensuring a total "mastery" of the "*Route of Druidism*" for this *Mardukite Master Course*.

The first installment—DRUID'S HANDBOOK—is a primer to Druidic fundamentals, clearly introducing key concepts and ideas developed for the Druid paradigm that remain relevant throughout the greater whole *The Druid Legacy* as explored throughout the remaining units of study. Yet, before even doing that, a *Seeker* is encouraged to carefully read through any introductory forewords provided.

Once you have familiarized yourself with the basic premise of Druidry, then proceed with a study of the ELVENOMICON material—which a *Seeker* will discover is actually a composite of three separate books in itself: one intensive unit of study that advances upon the foundations of the DRUID'S HANDBOOK and the legacy of Druidism in ancient European traditions, followed by two practical "grimoires" of "magical application." To receive the most practical benefit from the DRACONOMICON, it is important to have mastered a full working knowledge of the former material—as the information provided in DRACONOMICON and supplemental *Pheryllt Researches* are dependent on the provided foundation to be most effective as education and for practice.

There are many common points that bridge the *Route of Druidism* with *Grade-II* material pertaining to Mesopotamia, Babylon and Anunnaki. This is increasingly evident as a *Seeker* works successively through this material, finding origins for the Elven-Faerie traditions, symbolism of the Dragon and deeply hidden links to an original and archetypal Mystery School—all pointing toward the *Ancient Near East*, of which is explored extensively in *Grade-II*. When fully understanding the deepest teachings of the *Route of Druidism*, the direct relevance to the structure and Standard Model of *Grade-III Mardukite Systemology* will also become apparent!

: LECTURE 13—THE DRUID SCHOOL :
(September 23, 2020)

[*Okay, good morning! And this is September 23, 2020. And we're dealing with Route-D of Grade-I of the Mardukite Master Course. We're about half way through our first week of instruction. We've planned this course as a two week course; going through the complete Master materials. I know we had some visitors the second half yesterday, and I just want to remind everyone—I think they're no longer here—but, we were playing back the recordings from yesterday, last night, and noticed some electronic interference, so if you could make sure to put your phones on "airplane mode" if they're not already "off." Okay.*]

The course that we are dealing with now—a part of the course—*A Master Course in Druidry for Modern Druids*. The main textbook for this material is *Merlyn's Complete Book of Druidism*—and we went through, a couple days ago, what is contained in here real briefly. But, you can either use the Master Edition or we've actually released the individual books that are contained in here as well. Each is an anniversary collector's hardcover edition: *The Druid's Handbook*, what's now the *Elvenomicon* (what was the *Book of Elven-Faerie*) and the *Draconomicon*.

And then the—*Merlyn's Complete Book of Druidism* also includes the section on my "Pheryllt" research and then of course, the Master Course section that is also in your "Instructor's Manual." And you will see in the back there, we have a curriculum outline to Grade-I materials as they pertain to the "Route of Druidism."

What I thought I would do, since we are blending the Master Course into one conglomerate of knowledge—presentation—we've already been kind of talk about magick, ritual magic; yesterday, we started talking about "elemental magick" as a bridge *into* the study of Druidism, and so, what I want to do is kind of deal more with the practical mystical magical side of it first, so that we can move into some of the background and history towards the end of our time with the Druid material. And then as a result of that, it will bring us closer and closer into looking at Mesopotamia, where we will end up in Grade-II, when we are treating the "Route of Mesopotamia" specifically.

Now, the arrangement of this curriculum outline is actually new. This is something that we developed once I was setting out an outline for a full Master Course using the materials of the last twenty-five years that I've developed. So, I was trying to structure how to relay all of the portions of what's in *Merlyn's Complete Book of Druidism* now, in a concise way that would match with the other materials—with the... for example, being able to cross-reference with the *Arcanum* material, you can easily do that.

You can either teach out of the course material as it stands —as it's outlined in the back there, which is a chronology of basically the *Druid's Handbook*, the *Elvenomicon*, then *Draconomicon*. Now, in the past when portions of this was released as the *Druid Compleat*, these three sections were actually mixed and matched back and forth; sometimes it would start with *Elvenomicon* material; sometimes it would start with the *Druid's Handbook*. Sometimes the *Draconomicon* was in the middle; and in this instance, we've decided to close with it.

Of course the sequence of this: *Draconomicon*, I started developing in 1995, and *The Druid's Handbook* went through several different revisions before it was prepared in 2000 and then again in 2001 for the underground; and then several years after that I released the first "beta edition" of *Book of Elven-Faerie*, which is now the material in *Elvenomicon*. So, that was the sequence in which I laid it out. From *Elvenomicon*, I went directly into developing the *Arcanum*.

Really, when we launched Mardukite Ministries in 2008, the only real material there was the "Merlyn Stone" work, like the *Sorcerer's Handbook*, the *Arcanum* and then the "Druid" material. Really, it was the *Book of Elven-Faerie*, the history and background and presentation of Druidry in that, that really formed the link or bridge or attracted attention to the "Mardukite" system, because at the time, I was very unpopularly—back in 2008 and prior to that—basically explaining the origins and derivation of the Druid tradition *from* the Ancient Near East, and particularly Mesopotamia; and this was not a very popular concept at the time.

It's *still* not really popular *now*—but we actually have a lot more historical evidence and other lore to support it. Although for me: that's more for those that really need that background and confirmation—it doesn't change what it *is* on these *facts.*

There's so many complimentary point between, for example, treating a "Wizard School" and the *Sorcerer's Handbook* and *Arcanum*, and then also treating a "Druid School" as separate from that—because obviously we are treating it as two different "routes," there's two different textbooks here of material for each. But they *do* overlap and... as I explained at the very beginning, the "Master Course" and the presentation of the material as it's been published over the last twenty-five years follows along my own chronology as well...

So, given the fact that my involvement with Druidism stems from the same time period that I first was getting involved with practical magic, ritual magic, ceremonial magic also—1995—and so my involvement with Druidism coincided synchronously with my pursuits of general "magick" studies. There's a lot of cross-reference; you can definitely build upon the material, or emphasize material, from "Route-A" in like *Arcanum* that has to do with Druidism as a bridge. Or, for example, there may be individuals—depending on how you set up your Academy or your apprenticeships with your

Seekers—there may be individuals that are attracted more specifically *to* Druidism, the Dragon Legacy, Celtic Faerie Elven Traditions, that are less concerned with the styling and pursuit of traditional ritual magic.

We're not necessarily enforcing that, however, for example, in this Mardukite Master Course, I'm going to be discussing —we're going to deliver—the concepts behind Druidism and the materials that are in *Merlyn's Complete Book of Druidism* in light of the fact that we have already spent several days already talking about backgrounds and "magick" and some of these correlating points.

And that's one of the reasons why some of the works this way actually cover more ground; that's one of the reasons why this Master Course is considered a little bit more prestigious or profound than some of the other—even individual —collected deliveries or anthologies that I've been able to prepare over the years. Because we are looking at a wide span of knowledge and material here all at once.

Of course, we can only focus on, for example, at this point we're dealing with "Route-D," which is particularly "Druids and the Dragon Legacy"—Western Europe—however, this is not something that's exclusive to just one or another paradigm and it's all-encompassing. And that was one of the points behind even *Great Magickal Arcanum* originally, rather than just that "A-to-Z Encyclopedia" style, but that so much more ground could be covered assuming that ground is covered elsewhere; or that certain points can be applied to a wider range of studies that don't need to be repeated each time. And so we've been able to cover a lot more ground this way.

The point here being that sometimes it is hard to strictly draw a line between what would be purely applicable to your "Wizard School" versus what would be purely applicable to a "Druid School." I mean, I've simplified by presenting two different textbooks and two different collections of knowledge for that; but again, if you're running this as like a cumulative sequence of course or routes toward the *Pathway to Self-Honesty* into higher grades, then of course, you are going to want to focus on any of these points of connectivity; and especially be aware of the interest level that your Seeker has concerning any of the cultural associations that involve Western Europe, European Traditions, Western Magical Traditions and specifically Celtic Druidism.

My own personal background in Druidism is really only known in probably some select circles; it's commented on in some of the introductions and forewords of the materials that have been published. However, I've always been obviously been better known for the presentation of the "Mardukite" system, the "Necronomicon," my emphasis on Mesopotamia in the last decade or so.

But that wasn't what I was originally known for. In fact, when I was doing the work as "Merlyn Stone," the *Sorcerer's Handbook* was an application of "general" practical magick, not specific to one paradigm or another. It did cover elemental magick and Druidism, but it also covered other form of general "spellcraft" and the practices of ritual magic and neopaganism as they're observed in the New Age.

What really started it all—I was pretty much innately involved in "Nature" and "magic," "mysticism," elements of "fantasy," that was innate to me from prior existences and just being *who* I am. Really the only thing that I've spent time doing, I would say in the last twenty-five years, is really just honing the semantics about the types of things that I've already had an innate grasp on—and the ability to communicate those, the ability to research and reference history and actually bring some *reality* on it to other individuals, through what's become quite a prolific, I guess, "career" of writing.

And also delivering workshops and lectures... mostly "behind-the-scenes." This is one of the first times we're actually recording anything or delivering anything that's been outside of just the "underground" or my presentations *in* the "underground."

In 1995, I discovered—well, it's actually quite controversial in some respects and in some circles, but at the same time a lot of those politics have kind of simmered out from the '90s. Druidism is a—I mean, we might as well have called this lecture "Druid Politics" or something [*laughs*] because I have found it to be one of the most rigid, political, controlled and just very fixated traditions in the New Age, unfortunately—for all of its pursuits of "Truth" and "Universiality" and supposed acceptance... there's really a lot of politics and propaganda and stringent control over the mainstream presentation of "neodruidism."

This is usually not seen too much on the surface, because on the surface, modern Druidism is seen to be a very, almost, quasi-... fluffy, "Earth Wizard" almost "hippie" "naturefolk"-type... "environment..." It's actually quite a stringent study in terms of history, semantics, vocabulary, the lineages of traditions—all of this plays a real big part on what is considered "acceptable" for inclusion *in* modern "Celtic Druidism."

That even phrase being something I tend to lean away from. Now, it is very true that a lot of "Celtic" elements and "Celtic mythology" and "Celtic culture" *is* an integral part of what we know today as "Druidism." A lot of that pertaining to the fact that: here we have a system or a tradition that was very loosely cataloged along its ascent to become what it is.

There isn't a lot of *real ancient* written records for us to refer to. Now, there *are* medieval manuscripts, plenty of Welsh manuscripts, Irish manuscripts—all of these documents that were developed really within the last five-hundred years concerning the traditions, the Bardic traditions, all of the lore and "triads" and so forth; but again, these have actually been collected and composed within the last five-hundred years. We're not dealing with some 2000 or such year old tablets in this respect.

One of the falsehoods was that the Druids wrote nothing down. That's something that was professed mostly by the Roman accounts and if you look at the histories, you'll see that Celtic society and specifically the Druids which held the leadership and systematization and were the backbone of strength *for* the Celtic society in Europe—it's main *opponent* in its evolution, its culture, its growth, its ability to retain history to present day, was the Roman Empire.

As you see the Roman Empire build its strength and expand, it sought to eradicate not only Celtic culture, but most specifically, the Druids—they found the Druids to be virtually their archenemy. And it is unfortunate that the only accounts from that period of time that we have access to—scholarly and academically at least—*are* from Roman hands; they're Roman accounts. They are written *against* their enemy. It's very difficult for us to actually use those records as any kind of credible source for our picture and our perception of what ancient Druidism actually is.

When I bring up the "politics" of modern Druidism and NeoDruidism, it is not to scare you—it's simply to reinforce without making it a lot of negative statements or connotations about the movements, to reinforce my own decision to not "found" or "base" the delivery of our work from a "Druid School."

I've even only carefully employed the concept of a "Wizard School" or a "Magic School"—but again, even though I do have quite a bit of material, we have almost an entire grade worth of material in *Merlyn's Complete Book of Druidism* for that, I've never tried to emphasize the delivery of a "Druid School." The Mardukite Academy is simply, if anything, a Master School or a Syst... you know, the Academy of Systemology. It's all-encompassing.

If we were to "brand" it as a "Druid School," it would probably attract a different caliber of attention than we are really going for here. However, it's quite interesting, again, that really those were originally involved with the founding of "Mardukite Ministries" were *also* very impressed by, or influenced by, the concepts or the themes—even if not the literal statements or historical beliefs—concerning two of the more controversial aspects that, of course, become quite paramount in the Mardukite Academy or our tradition of knowledge.

These were: *The 21 Lessons of Merlyn* by Douglas Monroe; and Simon's *Necronomicon*—and so, although both of those materials an inspiration to, not necessarily the actual material or the actual work that I deliver, but the presentation *of*, the flavor *of*, the theme *of*. And so, as "beacons" it was really those that were finding interest in both of those, or had long-standing interest in both of those elements, that became the original founding members and part of the developments in the research organization back in 2008 and 2009 and 2010 and so forth.

Now, I was 12 years old at the time—and of course being as tenacious as I was today—I think I had the *21 Lessons of Merlyn* for a few months before I was basically in contact with its author, Douglas Monroe. And so, therein began a somewhat behind-the-scenes underground involvement with what was going on at the time. I saw this, that Druidism had a presence again, I understood it innately, I had a connection with "Merlyn" since childhood and it was very easy to fall into this regimen and this theme; this cultural setup of Druids, the cloaked Wizards and Nature-Priests and forests and hills and animals and all this.

This was all good stuff to me. So I went into it pretty much wholeheartedly and within six months had established basically my own—it was called the "Mystics of the Earth" and it was a study-group in Minneapolis actually, dedicated to the Druidic Mysteries. This ended up evolving into the "Draconic Celtic Lodge of Druids," which I established online for a brief period and then became the "Elven Fellowship Circle of Magick" once I was reestablished in Denver. That actually became a part of the high school there.

And so a lot of those materials—and a lot of that time period was spent—really focused on Druidism. Although the *Sorcerer's Handbook* was a publication that was quite popular and it was actually the original "Book of Shadows" and training guide for magick *for* the "Elven Fellowship Circle of Magick," I was still doing a lot of behind-the-scenes Druid work.

At the time, I was also considered the *youngest* member to have joined the "Order of Bards, Ovates and Druids" in England. Although, it's actually been handed over since—actually *this year*, the Chief has just handed it over to new leadership—but since 1988, that was run by a gentleman named Philip Carr-Gomm. So, I was actually involved with them for a couple years *until* it became known that I was actually involved with Douglas Monroe's operations.

Apparently, because of, again, solely the idea that Douglas Monroe had presented his material as "Authentic Druidism" (quote; unquote), it was being highly scrutinized and just attacked for really that reason, by virtually every "mainstream"—not necessarily the ones underground or ones with long-standing relationships with other underground streams—but mainstream Druidism.

And at the same time—*The 21 Lessons of Merlyn* remains to be the bestselling book on the subject of Druidism in modern times.

Now, as a representative—I mean, *you* represent the Mardukite movement when you use the materials, when you use or set up your courses, when you begin, like if you go on to be "Pilots," to process individuals—it's important for you to be aware of some of these elements because you are going to be out in the world dealing with it; having to confront and deal with the networking, the social medias, the individuals—whatever they're going to be, even if you're not, the people that you are interacting with may be out there doing various research and of course anybody can virtually say anything now on the internet and it's considered, you know, part of research or... it's not even being validated or, you know, cited properly.

It's just important to know this background when you're going to be dealing with this material, because as controversial as it might seem to the mainstream world or surface world, dealing with magick or mysticism or the occult in any way shape or form—within the "magickal community," within "New Age" movements, one of the more colorful elements that's found and inspires emotions and beliefs and opinions *is* Druidism. So, it's important to be aware of these aspects going into it.

Probably one of the more famous or one of the more commonly encountered points of contention concerning—well, beyond even my own presentation of the Mesopotamian origins [*laughs*] of Druidism—but the concept of the "*Book of Pheryllt*."

"*The Book of Pheryllt*" was this concept used to basically represent the collected wisdom of Welsh Druidism and the Bardic Tradition as it was presented in the works of Douglas Monroe. The material went on to be used for his other works, *The Lost Books of Merlyn*. The first two being published by Llewellyn publications. The third and final book in the Merlyn trilogy—which actually included several pages of an essay that I had actually supplied for the book specifically—the *Deepteachings of Merlyn*, which was released by Kima books (a small independent press out of South Africa).

To commemorate his final completion of the trilogy... It became clear to me, although those of us working close to his operations and his underground movement were aware of his travels—extensive travels—that a lot of people don't know about in terms of Britain and the areas looking for these manuscripts, looking for records, relics; all times of stuff to validate for himself, the presentation of the works that he delivered. Because he really didn't do this for popularity. He was actually do this to share something.

And I totally respected that... but it became very clear to me that he was not going to at any point release a "facsimile" or "verbatim" edition *of* the "Book of Pheryllt" (something that people had been long anticipating). I certainly didn't feel comfortable overstepping and getting in there and, you know, copying out microform [microfiche] pieces—it became clear to me that to solidify not only the work that he was doing but also to connect... it had long been known that there was a connection between Douglas and myself, in terms of the development of my work and the development of traditions. It was time to kind of kick that the other way.

So, I began in... oh, jeez, was it 2014? I think it was 2014, I began working on these volumes to make up the "Book of Pheryllt."* And this was meant to be a facsimile; it wasn't meant to be "Oh, *this is* the Book of Pheryllt that he keeps records of" or anything verbatim. But, I had been around enough to pick up enough of the themes and the concepts and what the elements were that this was all entailing to present such a facsimile.

And by that I mean, again, it's not pseudoepigrapha—the only point of contention being of course the name [title]. And rather than saying or even making the claim that the three volumes that I ended up compiling for this—which is part of the "Pheryllt Researches" in *Merlyn's Complete Book of Druidism*—these were not meant to be presented as the "Book of Pheryllt" verbatim as the "hidden book." But it was meant to be kind of a play—a literary play on—it is the book *of* Pheryllt, and it is the material that would be studied within the "Book of Pheryllt."

---

*   Now compiled into *"Draconomicon Vol. 2: Pheryllt Researches."*

The "Pheryllt Researches" made an excellent companion piece. It's not only the "Merlyn Trilogy" that *he* presented; but also to bridge into the work that I had been continuing independent of that. Because I should point out: the New Forest Centre and Mardukite Academy or Mardukite Ministries—they are two separate identities. The only point being that I do *cite* and *reference* and refer people to his work, in regards to "Druidism" *and* the New Forest Centre, which he operates.

I mean—*I'm* a member of it, but they have no sway of... as far as what we are doing here. I'm considered the "Bard of the Twelfth Chair." There's a virtual, basically, a "round table council" at New Forest and there's thirteen seats...and I'm considered the Twelfth Chair.

But they *are* two independent entities, except for the fact that the "Book of Pheryllt" was meant to be incorporated into their library; my facsimile of it. And so, what we ended up doing—since his third book was released through Kima Global, we ended up having "The Book of Pheryllt" released there as well. The reason being, I had always had this ambition of sharing a publisher with him, and developing some kind of companion work of this nature—I was anticipating a little bit more of a "chapter-by-chapter" study guide type thing, but this actually worked out quite well. And given that it was clear that he wasn't working with Llewellyn anymore, it was *much simpler feat* to essentially get "The Book of Pheryllt" published through Kima Global to give it a little more recognition and to coincide with his release of *Deepteachings of Merlyn*, which again, had included my own writings and credited as such.

So, that was actually kind of an exciting pinnacle there. His —*The 21 Lessons of Merlyn* was released in '95 [*err. 1992*]; *Lost Books of Merlyn* was released in '98 and it was actually not until 2011 that *Deepteachings of Merlyn* was released. And, I would say how disappointing it was for me that it took so long for it to reach publication—except for the fact that by that point, I was already a little bit more established and able to actually contribute something to that volume. So, that was a kind of... another exciting peak point in terms of my actual "career" aspect of this.

I don't really do this for the "glory" and "name recognition"—it's just that these confirmations are kind of indicative that, you know, that this has gotten some solidity and built some momentum over the years; and that this is actually going somewhere.

: LECTURE 14—DRUID FUNDAMENTALS :
(September 23, 2020)

In 2018, when we were anticipating the public inception—because we had been working underground for a decade—but the public inception of Systemology down the road, I released what was the "tercentenary" edition of the "*Pantheisticon of John Toland.*" And this material is now actually included in *Merlyn's Complete Book of Druidism*, and also in the "Master Course Instructor's Manual."

It's kind of an interesting anomaly of work. And it's kind of funny [*laughs*] I mean, everyone just kind of rolled their eyes when I first delivered this because here I am; I'm publishing "Necronomicon" books, I got the "Draconomicon," "Elvenomicon," "Cybernomicon"... all this stuff. Okay, [*laughs*] "Pantheisticon"—I didn't come up that one; that's literally the name of his booklet; and it's curious that the main woodcutting image of John Toland is actually of him—a bust shot—of him standing with that book... for as little as it's known.

Now, for those of you that aren't aware: John Toland, in 1717, established the "British Circle of the Universal Bond." That was the original inception and revival of "Druidism" that we can trace modern Druidism back to. There's *always* been scholarly... and little grove schools... and secret societies throughout history that have held a claim to that name. But in terms of the modern revival—in terms of what has led us up to what we can trace modern Druidism back through, for at least three hundred years—it goes back to Toland.

In 1726, he released "History of the Druids," which is actually a series of letters that were commissioned by a "Lord" of... at the time. So, such things—I mean, at this time in Europe—in England—publishing was kind of more of a, I don't want to say "vanity," but it was a prestigious thing, and it was often times commissioned or paid for by certain wealthy courtsman.

And so, in this respect, one of his most famous contributions—at least as is cited in the Druidic revival—is "History of the Druids" and it's essentially just an account of what was known or discovered or considered in terms of the philosophy and religion of the Celts and the Druids at the time.

This kind of concept of "learned men"—"learned beings"—who would gather together and discuss these intellectual and historical matters, became quite popular. At the same time in 1717, and at the same Apple Tree Tavern, we see a revival of British Freemasonry and the Premiere Grand Lodge of England founded. And so, this is a critical time period for the establishment of what is considered "esoterica" or the "esoteric lodge," the "esoteric brotherhood"—the "secret society."

Now, obviously the term "Pantheisticon," or the title, begs the question or calls to mind the term "pantheism." And it's interesting because "pantheism"—it's thrown around a lot now in philosophy and the "New Age" and various literature—but it's actually... John Toland is the first one to coin this term for his *Pantheisticon*. It was really meant to describe the paradigm of the philosopher Spinoza, which identified "God" or "Divinity" with the whole of the universe—All-as-One.

We see this kind of "secret doctrine" and the concept of "Universal Law" that animates and acts upon things relevant to the style of esoteric truth that's taught in the *Pantheisticon* and what later came from that. Yes, John Toland founded the British Circle of the Universal Bond, which later sprung, like the Ancient Druid Order and all these other—what they were considered "mesopagan neodruids."

But the purpose of the *Pantheisticon*, when you really analyze it, it's actually a "(secret) society" handbook, and it differentiates the concept of the "*esoteric* knowledge" from the "*exoteric* knowledge." That which is known or understood by a few, versus the kind of common denominator of knowledge that would be, for example, taught in schools or treated in the mainstream.

And so this is, I mean, this is a time before the "New Age" movement, this is a time before mass-publishing, this is a time even before the arrival of, for example, the Theosophy schools and the Orders of the Golden Dawn and so on and so forth. And what this actually was doing was setting down a guideline for the independent, but also within groups, pursuit of treating "learned knowledge" and "esoteric" and ancient knowledge, that would be only treated within the confines of a society—for example, this "secret society."

Not that there was anything [*laughs*] necessarily bad going on within it—or any other reasons for it to be so exclusive—but again, "esoteric knowledge" being that knowledge which could be shared, exchanged and developed, basically in the "underground" or the underbellies of the "surface world," which would not be necessarily ready to confront such information. This isn't the kind of stuff that you could just easily go and talk to "Joe" or "Bill" or "Mary" or "Sue" or something that's sitting on the corner bus-bench or at your local church, you know?

In order to protect the integrity of the individuals—in order to be able to have a forum and a medium of being able to relay and exchange these ideas and discuss—and this is basically what the "secret society" and "Druidic fraternities" and the original "Sorority-Motherhoods" and such, were based on, long before the concept became reduced to, for example, what we consider the "fraternities" and "sororities" at your local college or university.

The original purpose of these *was* for individuals to be able to remove themselves from the scrutiny or the biases or the ignorant opinions of the masses, to hone and develop their personal intellect; their academic pursuits—which of course, they were being specially trained and educated in... that was what differentiated them as "academicians," as "academy students"—as those that were moving up these levels or grades.

And so, even in Druidism, we do see the similar threefold, kind of "grade style" of education—a graded system in which different aspects are treated that would be given a specific emphasis or rank or title, and then of course represented differently—if we want to get into that now—you have the "Ovates" that are the new initiates or novitiates [*laughs*] that are coming in and learning as apprentices—they're new, they're green; they wear green; they spend a lot of time in Nature; they spend a lot of time (in) one-on-one apprenticeships *in* Nature, dealing with the trees, the plants, the herbs, the animals... learning from observation of Nature.

This then moves into the Bardic Grades—which are a little more academic: you're dealing with rigorous pursuits of "triads" and "doctrines" and other "skills" (and) "creative arts"—whether it's gonna be poetry, writing, music... history, and then they were traditionally known also as the musicians—and when we refer to the "wandering bards," they were the news-carriers and messengers. And so all of which were also participants in *this* Order—the Druid Order.

So, when you have these various grades like this: there was a way of structuring the organization; there were also Councils; there were various Colleges—Bardic Colleges—set up in various locations *and* there was a certain standard that was established. Much like going to school today, when you consider, like, an "Associates" or a "Bachelors" or a "Masters" or a "Ph.D."

These graded curriculums were very comparative to what we would consider standard education today, in that if you were going to be a physician, or you were going to be a lawyer, or you are going to be involved in the "civics" or the government, or some kind of specialized skill, you were gonna go to school for that—and you're going to be trained by the Druids and honed within the Druidic Colleges and the Bardic Colleges and trained in the arts of reading and writing and so forth, because this was something not always found among the common Celt.

And you see the same thing again in Mesopotamia, where you have a priesthood or a systematic tradition of culture that is basically represented by those who know how to read and write—and are the lore masters, the keepers of history and so forth—that have a higher access to a higher understanding than the common person; and for that, given positions of leadership.

That is really the kind of leadership that we see in ancient Celtic society when you look up just the generic concept of what a "Druid" is in a dictionary or an encyclopedia, it seems to emphasize, you know, "Celtic religion" and "Druid priests" and "priestesses" and so forth—but really, it had to do with the "learned echelon" of society that was "skilled" and "specialized" in their knowledge, or would go on to serve other functions in that society. And that's why the Druids are referred to as the "systematizers of the Celts."

Much like we'd see today, pretty much, the Druids would be anyone involved with civic duties, anyone involved with government, anyone who works with the state—even the postal carriers, teachers, educators, lawyers; virtually anything that you would have to go for a degree to accomplish in today's society, you would be a Druid in Europe, you know, thousands of years ago—that would be your title.

So these may seem... they're like basic fundamentals that I'm giving to you; but they are actually *not* arbitrary. When you look into the section of *Merlyn's Complete Book of Druidism* or the *Druid's Handbook* that deals with the "doctrines" of Druidism, most of these have to do—when people think of "doctrines" they tend to think of some kind of crazy religious law or beliefs or something. [*laughs*]

These actually have to do primarily with instruction; how to manage instruction, apprenticeships, degrees—applying a practical philosophy to the manner in which an individual is going to learn, attain and achieve mastery... which is kind of actually inherent to what we are doing here in the Master Course. It's essentially *learning* how to *learn*; learning how to evaluate. These are individuals in ancient times, thousands of years ago, which became the natural philosophers; which charted the first points of fact and the first directions of interest that became later schools of philosophy and the physical sciences of today.

We've only become more detailed and more specific as time has gone on, in terms of how many factoids we can develop about the Physical Universe; but the basic principles behind intellectualism, the academics, cosmology, astronomy... these were set down thousands of years ago, for all the efforts that modern academics like to go back and look at these time periods and likes to look at them as "savages."

Now, the "common man" may have not had an academic or intellectual handle of everyday world sciences—the physical sciences—as we might see today, mainly because of the differences in education, the availability of medias; I mean, even if you were to look back one-hundred years ago, before the television, before the widespread use of, like, the radio, the internet or any of these modern publishing... access to so much information now—the information age, you would see that the average individual, especially in a rural community, really was only concerned with what was right in front of them; and that these higher ideals—these higher pursuits—didn't really play much of an effect on what their everyday life consisted of.

So, you really only see—up until recent times, and then of course the widespread or marketed presence of all these "secret societies" and "lodges" and "Hermetic Orders"—you really see this stuff, kind of "confined" to specific graded "mystery schools" and "priesthoods" and "sororities" and "underground clubs" for thousands of years. And of course, this has inspired a lot of thought concerning conspiracy and other matters today—and of course, such networking could just as easily be abused, just as we might see today.

But its original intent—for example, some of the Rosicrucian schools and the original Masonic schools, you know—those that were participants in these were those that became, in public, known as the "inventors" and "innovators" and "philosophers" and famous writers that innovated and shaped the large directions and changes of culture—and the shifts in intellect, new capabilities, new technologies. These have always kind of come from the underground and the underbelly.

And it's even sometimes right in plain sight, just because some factory or some corporation may have some huge building and obviously they're not hiding the fact that the huge building... most of the work, all of the innovation, the research and the development—a lot of this becomes the most securely guarded, cut-throat... even people losing their lives over: "Mystery." ...concerning any kind of formulas or anything before it can be presented, you know, final form or packaged and patented, you see?

This is an ongoing thing.

So, when you're introducing these "doctrines," you're basically relaying—not so much the Chief Doctrines of Druidic tradition as given as a "code of laws" or religious semantics, but the formation of the Druidic Order. And not just the Druidic Order as a physical construct or a meeting of people, but the Druidic Order as in the "ordering" and systematization of the Celtic people with this methodology.

One of the things we see also is a "Doctrine of Separations." This has been misconstrued as some kind of "gender bias," but what we actually see is really an ancient origin for, again, that division between a "fraternity" and a "sorority"—particularly in educational parameters, because it's been noticed, of course, when you're blending "boys and girls" in a traditional public school setting that a lot of those dynamics and of the teasing or the "mystery"—a lot of those interpersonal relationships, which should be encouraged, it's not a pure separation—it's the fact that you would separate "boys and girls" for instruction simply to maintain the proper flow of attention.

So, when you enter in the equation of a "separations" or any of these *doctrines*, you're starting to deal really with Systemology. You're starting to deal with an early predecessor to *our* Systemology as it was treated in ancient Celtic

In this sense, you're talking about the flow of attention, you're talking about the reception, projection, of energies—we're talking about "Master-level" intellectual academic pursuits here—so, obviously we were concerned with getting the highest level of effectiveness in the material. Now, obviously we don't... for example, in the Academy *here*, there's both males and females present... Obviously this isn't a huge thing to be enforced; we're specifically talking about a Druidic methodology.

The *Druid's Handbook*—before it was called the *Druid's Handbook*—was actually a thesis that I was writing called *Applied Druidology*, and it was meant to be more on the "academic" level; and you see this kind of carried into the work and like the *Great Magickal Arcanum*, where it's being treated more with the semantics of philosophy and science and the "academics" that you might pursue at a college level, as opposed to the more elementary and basic rudiments of ritual magic and occultism that I obviously was exploring prior to that.

My own development—my own gradients, my own pathway —of course, is reflected in the delivery of the "Master Course" and the structure of, of course, *my perception* of the *Pathway to Self-Honesty.* It's not necessarily the *only* route; it's a route that *I've* found effective and, of course, *others* have found effective—particularly once you get into the higher echelons of the knowledge.

Another key principle, in terms of the "Druidic Doctrines," being the "Doctrine of Authority"—the accumulation of actual authority and the completion of cycles and gradients prior to the introduction of new ones; and that these gradients are meant to be built upon, such as in the framework of the "Ovate, Bard and Druid." You're building upon what has already been given; and this again, is part of that accelerated effective delivery of knowledge—kind of like what we do in the "Master Course," kind of like what *Arcanum* was intended as.

Otherwise, what you run into—without this standard—what you run into, and many people have found this in their education, even in modern times, is the lack of a standard or a constant repetition. "Well, I learned fractions last year at this other school and now I'm learning fractions again, or..." The curriculum is never geared toward these students, they're geared towards these arbitrary benchmarks that each teacher and each method, or each school, will have their own of. And so although there is a certain *basic* "frame" or "guide," you see these inaccurate and inappropriate methods of delivery in terms of education. You see this holding people back all the time in conventional education.

We may be dealing as a metaphysical school, or we may dealing with subjects of "magick" and we may be looking at alternative aspects of history that seem to be a little more hidden than others—but at the "Mardukite Master Course" level, given my twenty-five years of developing this, at least at this point, we're treating this work as a very serious academic and intellectual pursuit. Also an effectively practical one that can be employed and demonstrated because otherwise it's just a bunch of knowledge and data.

We are treating something very real here—and although it may be misunderstood... again, this is again why I chose not to make a specific "Druid School" or emphasize a "Druid Order" of my own in which to deliver the materials, I've simply integrated it into an all-encompassing "systemology," which we have just dubbed the "Mardukite" brand because of what it represents—the organization that has developed this work and what I've been involved with for now thirteen years, that is not specific just to interpreting "Mesopotamian" or something about a deity or Anunnaki god named "Marduk."

We're dealing with simply a paradigm now, that we've gone back to about as far as we can go in terms of "material mundane records" and have then synthesized this 6000 years of material that we can present as the "Mardukite Master Course" and then of course, extend beyond that with the futurist NexGen movement that we have as "Systemology," which we break into in Grade-III—even within the confines of the Mardukite (Master) Course.

So, that's a big element of that and that's part of also the "Mystery School"—the "Mystery School" which we talk about, of course, in the *Pantheisticon* material, in terms of what John Toland was establishing as a "Socratic Society" and there's a lot of details of that in there. And then the "Doctrine of Imbalances" being what we just discussed in terms of gearing the curriculum and the attentions of a Seeker—of a Student—towards the point of *weaknesses.*

This is not to mean "focus on what they're doing wrong." You give them *wins* and then focus to make sure there's a balance on the other aspects and work it up on a gradient scale, like you'd build a wall—like building a brick wall—you do it as evenly as possible; working on one (side) and then the other and working back and forth.

Concerning the "Doctrine of the Enlightened," well of course, it's been established that children—not having been subjected to as much programming and agreements with the Physical Universe yet, or have encountered enough pain and turbulence and various experiences that have restimulated or triggered other forms of fragmentation—obviously it was noted that they have a unique "learning" capability, which became crystallized—knowledge would become crystallized in an individual—as they would age, that things would become more static, fixed... masses would take more, well the beliefs and thoughts would turn into masses with heavy emotional charge given that a person would defend (it) as a "belief," they would literally kill or die for: the emotional mass that they would carry as beliefs concerning the outside universe. These are important principles just in the relay and presentation of "Druidism."

And then finally, briefly we'll run through what's considered the "Doctrine of the Spheres"—otherwise it would be known as the "Druid's Cabala." It's kind of related to the Welsh Bardic Tradition, but if you look very closely at what it represents, we are actually talking about the Standard Model here—the Standard Model of Systemology—and so here's another point in which you can actually very successfully incorporate the Standard Model of Systemology as an educational tool and as a bridge to higher levels of realization, crossing it with the information that we can pull—these "models" and "examples"—from these other gradients and traditions.

In this instance you have—well, in some respects they're called "Circles," but they should really be more considered as "Concentric Spheres" encompassing one another, which is in some respects, is what we represent the Standard Model of Systemology as.

So, in the first sphere, you have *Abred*—and this would be essentially the "Physical Universe" or "Realm of Matter," the home of the animal-, plant-, tree-, human- "kingdoms." The Sphere of *Abred* basically represents, at the center, what we were showing (or discussing) in the "elemental model" we were using yesterday, the "Physical Universe"—the continuity and condensed nature *of* the "Physical Universe," of which it has a very heavy gravitational pull.

And then of course, the concept of "transmigration," "reincarnation" or "rebirth" in the Druid Tradition concerns the reform or "Ascension" of the individual as a *being* to break and defragment the "pull" or "gravity" of *this* existence. And this is one of the ways in which, again, there are a lot of parallels... if you're looking for parallels of Systemology *in* "ancient tradition," you'll probably find more of them in Druidry and then again in Mesopotamia than anywhere else. And it's probably for (these) purposes and reasons that I chose to emphasize those two particular facets more than any other.

Beyond the Sphere of Abred, you have the second sphere—the "Middle Sphere"—of *Gwynedd* (or "*gwen-eth*") and this is actually... it's named the "White Place" and that this is, this is your—what's sometimes been considered as a substitute—the "Astral Plane" or the "Spirit Realm." But, it's basically the Alpha existence. *Abred* being the the beta-existence, material universe, physical conditions—and then outside of that being completely different sphere of existence, the Alpha sphere of existence.

And this is a completely different vibration or frequency of existence, much like what we represent in the Standard Model—this is not where you go to the edge, you know, the material physical edge of *this* "Physical Universe" and somehow reach a doorway or somehow a boundary and the next one beyond. They operate above the frequencies of each other so that they don't necessarily interact directly.

There's obviously points—when we consider the ZU-line for the Spirit or Self—there's points which these are interacted with: *Life* essentially being the point in which spiritual existence can essentially animate, take over and move that which is organic material existence. But otherwise, it's spatially—we're talking about two different things.

And finally, they also classify, much as we do, that there's this ALL—this encompassing ALL—which is a boundary point, either *All* that *is*, for example, everything that could be conceived would be the "White Space" and the *All* that *is*, being a boundary point essentially between the "Everythingness" and the "Nothingness"; the Infinity outside of which is "Nothingness."

This is the same model that we have in Systemology and it can be very easily represented within the Druid Tradition.

: LECTURE 15—DRUID PHILOSOPHY :
(September 23, 2020)

[*So now we'll cover a bit of the Druid Philosophy and some of the key points what is classified as "Druid Wisdom."*]

There are a lot of colorful elements of the Druidic Tradition —mystical, magical, the Celtic Faerie tradition, the Elven tradition, "tree magic"—all kinds of various colorful aspects that can be explored within a "Druid Academy" or "Druid School" and within a "Wizard School" or a "Magic School."

To differentiate what is specifically the intellectual and philosophical aspects of the Druidic mystery tradition or mysticism or the "Druid Path," we'll want to cover that just to make sure that everybody is on the same page concerning the fundamentals and the basic tradition of philosophy —the wisdom tradition—and this has been synthesized or codified in a series of, what's called, "Welsh Triads."

"Welsh Triads" are a form of Bardic "verse"—or poet... or writing style—that attempts to basically give a chronology or *schema* of a certain train of knowledge or a certain statement or a certain concept or idea. And... we'll just get right into these, because it's fairly easy to understand here...

For example, "Three Quests of Mastery: Master of Self; Mastery of the Physical; Mastery of the Unknown." So, you have the Three Quests of Mastery. The concept there being that the Three Quests of Mastery—that statement—encompasses the following three statements of the triad: Mastery of the Self; Mastery of the Physical; Mastery of the Unknown.

When you think of the Three Quests of Mastery, it already kind of, in it's title... so, there's *always* "three" as a mnemonic device; they were big fans of the mnemonic devices.

And then of course "Mastery" being the *key* of each one, so you have: Self, Physical and Unknown.

When you consider "Self," *self-discipline, self-knowledge, Self-Honesty*, the use of Willpower, exercising the influential power of the Mind—this is all connected to what we are striving for up at the very pinnacle of everything. So, *this* is first and foremost; and yet, and the same time—you got the Physical Universe; you got the Unknown—the whole point being that these three levels of Mastery are all actually encompassed within *one*.

Mastery of the Self and Mastery of the Physical and Mastery of the Unknown are actually *all* elements of the same "Mastery." And it's what we've been talking about with the "Master Course" that the emphasis on the "Unknown Mystery"—the "Unsolvable Mystery"—emphasis on agreements with the Physical Universe and further trying to compartmentalize knowledge of the Physical Universe and fragment it and structure it—these are all secondary to *Self*, and that *through* Self, of course, you know, "Man: Know Thyself, by Knowing Thyself, Know All."

These were all laid out within the basic structure, for example, of the Druidic knowledge or the Druidic Tradition of philosophy, of which has later been borrowed from and reused in countless applications or sources, but here in, you find the original root of it; which is of course, what we delve into for the purposes of the Western Magical Tradition—you're delving into the sources of Western Magical Tradition, you discover Europe, you discover Druidry.

You look into the origins of Western Europe or European traditions of Druidism and the traditions that spread and you find yourself in the Ancient Near East—in Mesopotamia. So, there's a logical sequence to how all of this is laid out for the Mardukite Master Course—and also just how it's laid out when *you have it all* laid out in front of you, which has never been successfully done before, in terms of a "Mystery

School" or an "Esoteric Class" or an Academy like this—the knowledge has always been fragmented into a particular paradigm or semantic-set as opposed to looking at the wider-angle view and seeing the big picture.

It's important to note though: wisdom and knowledge are two different things. Wisdom inherently within the Druidic Tradition is composed of true knowledge *times* experience *times* objectivity. And this is reflected in the triads such as: "The Three Virtues of Wisdom: To Be Aware of All Things; To Experience All Things; To Be Removed From All Things." And this is mirrored in the "Three Keys to Transcendence: See All; Study All; Experience All."

There *is* a different between wisdom and knowledge. There are people who have accumulated much knowledge without wisdom; wisdom without knowledge. Wisdom, for as much as is given a lot of spiritual weight, does not *always* represent any kind of effective practical *Beingness*. Wisdom is sometimes the result of an actual inability or unwillingness to actually *act* or *do* or *be* anything. It's almost a withdrawal *from*.

And there's nothing wrong with empirical observation or applying, you know, the methodology of "logics" and "structures" and accumulated knowledge; but what we of course found later on—if you look at the *key* here, it says "To Be Removed From All Things." The point being that there's a lot of data and knowledge that could be had. We could create an entire new field based on some particular *datum* or particular belief or postulate and create a whole semantic vocabulary around it and establish it as something to *know about*.

And that would still be considered "true knowledge" or "true" to the extent of that paradigm. That when we say this "word" or whatever and we've given it this definition and we apply it to the syntax of some language, we can represent that there's something to know about—and this is done with "invented knowledge" and new objects and things all the time.

Now, the "experience" of that—the experience there—being, of course, that there is some kind of reactive-response or impression implied. And so now, a person *has* an experience; and that experience could be "good" or "bad"—it could be "pleasurable" or it could be "painful"—and these are all considered "true" again to the perspective of *that* individual.

But, of course, now, if we are really talking about "true"—"*true knowingness*"—a wisdom that's effective or something that's going to actually bring you a state of transcendence, here the last point being of course, "objectivity." So, "To Be Removed From All Things"—the "objectivity."

The point there being—we are not talking about detachment in terms of a complete withdrawal; what we are talking about is an absence of reactive-response mechanisms and associative thinking and patterned-programmed, or even implanted, thoughts or patterns/conditions, which have an emotional attachment to them.

There again we find "Systemology" coming into play again. Because "To Be Aware of All Things," "To Experience All Things"... Experience in itself can be quite fragmentary—it's very "*aberrative.*" "Removing From All Things" *is* to basically "empty out" like we see even the Grade-III Systemology practices—the emptying out *of* emotional conditioning, emotional mass and weight and heaviness and gravity that is affixed to these things.

But again, if you go up to the very top: "To Be Aware of All Things," or in the case of the second triad, "To See All"— you're up at the very top echelon of knowledge again. See, the other one's are a whole pattern that seems to cycle back —and then if you were to just simply *Be* what it is you want to *Know*, you would have a direct line of knowledge; you'd have direct "*gnosis*" of whatever it is you're seeking knowingness of.

The other way around: where you're studying, experiencing and having to be objective and then remove all the conditioning and so on and so forth—is simply a longer "route." But, it's all, again, contained within the original ideal of the triad.

Then we get into the more "administrative triads" having to do with leadership, qualities of the council, education, the structure of the Druid Order and so forth—because again, this is a big part of the "Mystery School." And then you have the "Three Keys to Druidic Mastery: To Know; To Dare; and To Remain Silent," which we actually covered (yesterday).

Finally, the "Three Requirements For Druid Apprenticeship: Eyes That Can Truly See Nature; A Heart That Can Truly Feel Nature; Clarity That Can Truly Understand Nature." Really there, pointing out that Druidry being a very Nature-oriented path—a "Pathway to Ascension," of course—but inherently ingrained in Natural Philosophy, the observation of the natural world—the "Green World."

"Three Objectives of Bardcraft: Reforming Society; Ensuring Peace In The Land; Preserving the Excellence of the Earth." Of course, the Druids priding themselves on the ability to manifest change in the environment; to be at Cause in one's Reality and of course, having that higher echelon of *Knowing* and *Being*, they obviously had a greater understanding of basic "ethics."

"Laws" are implied *only* when people have a low Actualized Awareness levels; they are not maintaining high, what we would call, "Zu"-levels in Systemology or high levels of, quite simply, *Beingness*—the state of Self, the state of I-AM. They are occupying some other point-of-view or entrapped and convinced that they are in some lower conditions of existence and that *that's* all they can operate as. This leads to that more "dog-eat-dog" "Law-of-the-Jungle" "stomping over each other to try and achieve some kind of material success" or what's considered the matter or masses or resources of mundane survival *in exclusion* to all else.

Of course Druids operate... When we look at the "Spheres of Existence" in Systemology, we cap off the Human Condition at 4.0 (*four*). And then beyond that we talk about the Human Condition being inherent to a *fifth* Sphere of Existence on Earth, which is of course, *All Life on Earth*—being an inherent part *of* All Life on Earth, but All Life on Earth being a wider more encompassing Sphere of Existence, which a lot of individuals are completely out of touch with; they are going in the other direction still.

And then we come to the "Three Laws of Apprenticeship: A Master Can Only Take One Apprentice Per Degree At A Time; A Master Must Instruct Degrees Separately; Apprentices Cannot Take On Apprentices Of Their Own." Of course, this is a little bit different at the Academy or College level; we're talking about individual apprenticeships—but it is something that I actually *did*, I mean up until delivering workshops and courses such as this from whatever office I was working from, really this was something that I adhered to.

In this respect, a Master being like a "Third Degree" or "Third Grade" or "Third Level" Master taking only one Grade-I and one Grade-II initiate or Seeker on at a time; and then also not blending the two—not instructing the two at the same time—because obviously we're dealing with two different gradients of material here.

And this could be just as applicable to the gradients and degrees of our Mardukite Master Course or individual smaller applications, rather than the Academy, but your individual apprenticeships with Seekers, as it would be with the levels of Druidry.

And then of course at an Academy level, just as we talked about *covens* and *groves* and various factions or, you know, mocking up an example or version of the outline for the "Hermetic Order of the Crystal Dawn" that I had done—we talked about all that the last couple days—you could just as easily do something on a practical level within the Academy for your "Druid School," where you're essentially having the equivalent of a "student council" but operating as a "Druid's Council" for the governing of that class; "class" meaning the group of students at that time. As they move through the Grades, of course, that would differ.

It isn't that we're actually going to lose any of this as one goes on, we're just trying to get one *through* into the levels of Systemology where everything actually comes together— and you can actually achieve some highly effective results, and then whatever "practices" or, you know, inclinations has to operate, you know, within a Druid School or even become Masters or Instructors themselves, you know, they can go along and actually continue to do that.

That was one of the elements of the Druid Tradition—or the structure of the Druid Order—is that many did not dedicate their entire permanent lives to some, like as "clergy" or to live in a "monastery" permanently, that was just something that *was* available. Some of them would only achieve an "Ovate" or a "Bard" grade-level of education—or simply the education required for the "trade" or "skilled profession" that they were looking to go into, and then they would go off and live fairly normal lives; they would always be usefully a part of the Druidic Order unless [*laughs*] they were "excommunicated" for some reason.

There were many that would go off and get married and live traditional lives. Often times their children would be sent to the Druid Schools from a young age; as opposed to someone that might enter Druidry through some other fashion. So the tradition would be continued—and carried on—almost like a "family legacy."

And you see inherently with Druidry today this concept of "legacies" of "family legacies" and "tradition legacies" whereas these would have been carried on successively from parent to, you know, successive generations over a period of time; and therefore almost keeping the "Druids" as a separate faction of society, as almost a separate population or even race then the common Celt, which might have been made up of all different tribal backgrounds and so forth.

In addition to the triads, I mean, in terms of a "Druid Council" or a group or a *grove* or a *coven* or any kind of practical "circle-group" application *of* these traditions—there's plenty, I mean, between the materials in *The Great Magickal Arcanum* and the material in *Merlyn's Complete Book of Druidism*, I've almost completely lost count of the number of group applications, group liturgies, initiations, ceremonial seasonal rites—various ways in which a group of people can apply and practice and explore these principles; and fairly safely.

None of this is gonna—if it's guided by a proper Master—none of this is going to get into anyone into any trouble. The only thing about groups is the matter of group dynamics and that's another aspect of understanding high level of applications of even Systemology, in terms of the Human Condition.

In the triads we have "Three Foundations of the High Council: Truth In Our Hearts; Strength In Our Hands; Consistency In Our Tongues." You know, this is one of those plaques you could just kinda put up on a wall.

Another one, "Three Conditions For Losing A Chair On The Council: Performing Murder or Warfare; Telling A Falsehood In Council; Divulging Secrets Of The Council." Those are all fairly self-evident—self-explanatory.

And then: "Three Responsibilities of Right Judgment: Listening Openly; Answering Discreetly; Observing Mercy and Justice In Judgment." Again, this boils (down) to something we would explore in Systemology, in terms of application of high-level thought in...

You gotta look at... when you're examining ancient history —whether it be the Druids, Mesopotamia, anywhere where you see these high-level mystics and priest-classes—you're dealing with intellectuals and people that were able to probably conceive of things fairly closely to what we would use today in our Systemology; perhaps just not with as refined of vocabulary or as many examples or practical applications, for example, like the electronic devices we are starting to employ at higher levels of Systemology—and so, this is all stuff that crosses over and is why the Master Course can be given as such, because it's a wide-encompassing ordeal.

[*This is not just about "magick and mysticism." We'll get into some basic "Druid Tech" in our next lecture before the lunch break though... So, here's one...*]

"Three Influences Of A Person: What They Believe Themselves To Be; What Others Believe Them To Be; The Identity of Self." And so, right there, there's some [*laughs*] high-level Systemology for you, in terms of the acquisition of artificial "phases" or "personality programs" and the "packages" of "filters" and "point-of-views" that are attached with those.

A lot of this does boil down to that basic "Know Thyself" context; but, again, that's such a simple concept almost— and this is one of the things that gets lost in these later applications or later presentations you see in the New Age *of* these former "Mystery School" applications, because this stuff is not incredibly complex; it's been made complex, it's been made mysterious, it's been turned into "forbidden knowledge," it's been given labels by which to keep the majority of the individuals and the common masses and such *away*.

But these basic principles can be demonstrated to increase the quality of Life, and as a result of that, provide the *wins* necessary to encourage someone on that *Pathway to Self-Honesty*—because all of this is still leading upwards.

It's only really at the lowest levels that we are concerned with a Mastery of the Mundane and "taking over the earth" and stuff of that nature—"taking over our fellow man." As we start moving up in "levels"—the gradients of the Pathway—the higher gradients for even beyond the Master Course into the Wizard Levels, as ability and knowingness and beingness increases, the desire, the compulsion, the interest in this, like, low-level inappropriate enforced use of control—it actually kind of dissipates.

And that's why I say these principles demonstrate a higher level of ethics and a higher level of reasoning and thought that made policing amongst each other quite unnecessary. It was a *big* ordeal—a *big deal*—if someone was being excommunicated from the Druid Order, because these individuals were simply honed and developed and trained and had progressed to a point where such was just not—it just wasn't within their nature anymore.

Of course, here in this other triad, we have "Three Aspects To Keep In Check At All Times: The Hand; The Tongue; Desire." So what you're doing; what you're saying; and what you're feeling. Well, that just comes back to Self-Control and Self-Mastery again. This is all very good sense.

Now, the "Three Avenues of Active Imagination: The Way Things Might Be; The Way Things Ought To Be; The Way Things Seem To Be." I mean, there you've got... you know, anyone that's got any kind of creative blocks taking place, you just take any aspect of those elements and start creating—just use one of those themes.

"Three Aspects Avoided By The Wise:" (here again, we're approaching into Systemology) "Fearing The Inevitable; Expecting The Impossible; Grieving The Irretrievable." When you take a look at those—those are all based on "experience"; they are all based on either encoded emotional imprinting, or some kind of associated knowledge, you know, mental programming. But, they're all basically the conditions which are going to leave someone in a fragmented state. I mean, those conditions right there are exactly what we are *defragmenting* at Grade-III, right within the Master Course.

"Three Ways In Which A Person Is Measured:" (I mean, here you can apply directly to *Piloted Processing* and making assessments of a Seeker) "By Their Hopes and Ideals; By Their Fears and Issues; By Their Neutrality and Indifferences." And here—right there—you can measure the emotional reactivity and response aspects to any kind of "mental imagery" or "belief" or thought-pattern that an individual is carrying with them. So, you can start to look at—actually incorporate—higher-level Systemology in your "Druid School" right within many of these triads.

It's important to have that higher-level understanding *first*. It's one of the reasons why we don't really encourage people to branch off and form groups or, you know, start their own thing until they've actually gone through the Master Course and the Master Grade-level of materials. Because you can actually go back and incorporate a much higher, much more advanced, and much more effective, application of education to your Seekers or assistance even into *your* daily life by seeing the wide-angle picture here.

This is something we always knew when we were examining these triads back when we were working with them and publishing them with the "Mardukite Truth Seeker Press" before I started my own independent *Imprint*, but it's only been up until recently with the codification and development and completion of Grade-III "Mardukite Systemology" that we were able to go back and actually find all these points of reference that, "yeah, this is exactly what we've been after all along."

It's been set down there in print as a beautiful triad—but, again, because of the simplicity that all of this originated as, the complexity came in actually not because this stuff was so hard, but because it was failed to be understood and duplicated properly as time went on. And so, *more* was added to it; *more* different opinions and takes on it were incorporated; so it became kind of a convoluted mess, and all of the simple basics that were actually effective were overshadowed by a lot more "colorful" presentations or iconic imagery or symbols or what have you.

That was again one of the purposes of the "*Mardukite Master Course*," was to ensure—given that we have now, across these four volumes, I mean this is 3600 pages of Master Edition material for the three grades, not including what's just been excerpted from it to make your "*Instructor's Manual*," and then of course, when we finally put together some kind of "Transcripts" for all of these lectures that I've been giving—it's important that more than just reading through it verbatim, that someone has been able to *access* this wide-encompassing understanding...

...Because you *may* or *may not* get these higher-level realizations *just from* a straight "read-through" or isolated read-through of one or another of the books. It's all there; it's all been laid out. But again, if it's treated in isolation as, well, like "magick" versus "Druidry" versus something labeled "Necronomicon" or "Mesopotamia" versus "whatever this Syste..."

When someone has only been seeing it as these "separate" "factions" or "divisions" or "grades" or "presentations" that we've been putting out—and sees them as being something separate from one another—as opposed to being completely intertwined and incorporated into this cumulative "Master Course-level" of realization.

They may not get it all. ...And that's okay. There's books—they have the ability to be gone back over and reviewed again and used as research and study material. So, an individual can very easily go through one of these individual books even, even if they don't have a Master Edition—to go through, like, the *Druid's Handbook* or the *Elvenomicon* or the *Draconomicon*—they will find plenty of material this is of benefit to them at whatever grade or level of understanding they are at.

And then of course, again, once you start to incorporate more of this puzzle together—more of the pieces together—and to see this bigger picture and to be able to stand back and see more of the timeline stretching across before you, you can go back over those materials again, and you will actually find that they are relaying a whole new level of information. They've been designed that way. I've been... I mean, I intentionally designed them that way and really structured the way the literary work was presented.

It's going to be something that—well, why we put together these "keepsake" editions and the hardcovers and what not—it's going to be something that you refer back to and you're going to discover more that was there than you originally had experienced.

This is something that makes... I mean, these materials have been around with us now for ten, fifteen, twenty—in the case of the *Draconomicon*, twenty-five years. So, the relevancy and the standard which they actually put forth is not obsolete, and has actually only furthered the idea that this all integrative as a complete Mardukite Master Course because they do actually pick up and leave off and overlap and bring out in one another new levels of realization with each pass through them.

Before we get into any actual "Practical Druid Tech" and those elements of it, I just wanted to make sure—express here—that although it is intellectual and academic and what not, I didn't want to make Druidry seem too "stuffy," as opposed to some of the other elements out there—some of the other neopagan traditions—that seem to be just a little bit more "fun and fancy free" and emphasize more of the seasonal or cyclic or pagan traditions or customs or things that you could make or do or, you know, chant around bonfires, and so on and so forth.

But, I did want to at least impress the idea that above what you might consider as just this standard—this standard issue, you know, "gypsy fortune tellers" or the "rural village witch" or the "indigenous shamans" and so on and so forth—when we get to the point of Celtic Druidism, we are actually dealing with something that has been quite adamantly systematized, codified and put into a tradition that emphasized the intellect and academia and the pursuit of "true knowledge" and "universal truth" above all else.

It is at this point that we begin to see that "priestly" elements—the priests and the priestess and these ministers—not so much in the religious context that we might view them today, but that what they represented in the ancient world, was simply a learned—almost separate—class of citizen, that which operated on a level that the average individual was not at a point of reality with to understand.

: LECTURE 16—DRUID RITUAL TECH :
(September 23, 2020)

Throughout Grade-I there are so many different applications of "natural magic," the use of the "elements," the use of "natural surroundings," aspects or components that are taken from Nature: stones, sticks, you know, you name it, it's got a magical application or association or some kind of classification, in one of these traditions.

For that reason, the division between Route-A and Route-D, particularly applies to the actual traditions of Druidism, its origins as the "elemental magick"—the "Elven" and the "Dragon" traditions associated with that—but the actual, the effective techniques, the actual "Druid Tech," is not specifically only explored at a Druidic level in today's "New Age" and of course, in our Academy, it's no different.

The traditions of "magick" and a lot of the elements from that, which became popularized as Druidry was pushed "westward"—you know, it occupied all the way from the Ancient Near East through to what we know today—but as the persecution, the Roman invasions, various changes in culture and all that, the Christianization, all pushed it "westward."

We find that in part of France, and of course Britain and the British Isles—United Kingdom, Ireland, Scotland—these areas have a concentration of it that survived longer than the other geographies and parts of Europe. And so, it's not really surprising to see that the modern neopagan traditions—modern Wicca and Witchcraft, modern traditions of Druidism, modern Shamanism, a lot of the "Magical Orders" that have risen up in the last few hundred years and which are still quite prominent—have all actually developed *from* the final resting place there in Western Europe, even including places like Germany and such.

In doing any kind of "Magic Course," as I was pointing out in the beginning, or any kind of "Druidic Course," and especially when we get to Mesopotamia and beyond, you're not really able to separate it from history—from the study of history. A lot of people—they still have a lot of conditioning and fragmentation on the subject of "school" or on the subject of "learning" and their misemotion over the experiences they've had with the inappropriate handling of education—but really, the pursuit, if you were to present this as only "here is a historians club" or some such, you probably wouldn't get the same caliber of individual or the same drive of someone naturally looking for a point of Self-Actualization, or a "mystical" study or something that they can *do*.

A lot of these elements of history have actually *been* explored at academic levels and various universities around the world, and most of the time the students of such only come out talking like their textbooks—or having a vast ability to correlate or regurgitate various names and dates and places, but as far as an actual *applied* understanding or an *effective* workable, anything that they can actually *do* with it, most of them, it just becomes an intellectual or academic field and they continue to write their history books, but it doesn't seem to have any kind of effective application or... it doesn't seem to change the everyday man.

Even though the history books or what we know about it—I shouldn't say the history books, although people are publishing all the time; but the "textbooks," the standard knowledge of history doesn't seem to change what an individual is dealing with in their everyday life.

A lot of the things that we deal with in the Mardukite Academy that we kind of take for granted now in terms of the Anunnaki, in terms of past lives, in terms of things that sound very much like science-fiction or fantasy, you know, we just kind of accept because to *us* it all makes sense. To the average individual who is still very much clinging onto these other paradigms or other ways of reasoning, it may not necessarily make sense.

In terms of actually studying this stuff, I've tried to keep the "history" of the Druids kind of separate from our study of the "mystical" and "philosophical" aspects of it, so that we can incorporate it into Mesopotamia (for Grade-II).

Some of the most basic elements of "Druid Tech" are actually introduced in the *Sorcerer's Handbook*, and there's actually plenty more in *The Great Magickal Arcanum* that can be incorporated or cross-referenced into a "Druid School" or a "Druid Course." It doesn't necessarily have to be an independent school. We use that term depending on what an individual ends up doing with it, but you can also do what we do with the Mardukite Academy is offering various "courses" which emphasize a particular aspect.

In the *Sorcerer's Handbook*, I mean, I was already introducing —way before I was writing exclusively on Druidism—was some elements of, again, the "elemental magic" we were talking about (yesterday) and then the incorporation of Trees. Now, we'll be talking about the "Ogham" and "tree work" and "tree rituals" and such when we deal with the "Elven"—*Elvenomicon*—the "Elven Tradition" portion of the Master Course.

But, even at an introductory point, there's some things you could actually practice with. Having a Seeker—or even yourself—going to a special tree and... if you're a beginner, the one that I actually started with which seemed to work really well, was to use a Pine Tree or something with needles, so that you can put your fingers on the sharp needle ends and just hold them there and just kind of get that sensation of— kind of like an electrical flow, like when you meet somebody new and you touch, that kind of surge.

If you have skills in "imagery"—or you've already worked with them with skills, your Seekers, with skills in imagery—you can actually visualize like a white stream of energy flowing between the tree and you. When you work with "tree communication" in the advanced "tree work," you kind of do a similar thing; you try to tap into the "emanation" of the *Lifeforce*—what would be considered "ZU"—because it is a living being; it does have its own living circuit through it, and we don't even know what entity might have attached itself to it... that just might be sitting there as a point-of-view.

Trees have a long lifespan and can carry a considerable amount of *Earth Memory*, in terms of the changes in whatever its environment is. So, "trees" definitely have something to "say." [*Laughs*] Anyone that's had any kind of experience with Druidism or Elven Magick and the Faerie and things of that nature, know that there *is* a communicable relationship possible with Nature; and this relationship —this concept of "communing" with Nature—is a pretty inherent part [*laughs*] of any kind of "Druid Tech." That's pretty inherent in it—any of its "mysticism" or magic or traditions.

Trees are actually an excellent focal point, in terms of, for example, you have other kinds of ritualism and other tools and other things in, like, Route-A; and in Route-D, trees actually an make excellent focal point in terms of work, meditation, study, communing with Nature and other things. We'll deal other "tree work" and, I guess, "Tree Tech" we'll call it [*laughs*] a little farther on when we deal with forest traditions of the Elves and Celtic Faerie Tradition, but I just wanted to throw that out there as just a basic, you know, difference between the sense of what you're doing in a... what "Druid Magic" would be, I guess, in relation to "low magick" or "spellcraft" or "ritual magic" and some of the examples you would find in other applications.

Keeping with where we were talking (yesterday) about "Elementalism" and the "Elements," the "Druid Ritual Tech" that I've found most effective—and easily deliverable—is structured based on the "four elements." It has four "phases" and the Earth Phase, you're dealing with physical preparations; in the Water Phase, you're dealing with inner preparations; the Air Phase, the internal intentions are meeting the external environment; and then the Fire Phase, you're dealing with actual manifestation or actual handling of energies.

What I did—when I went through these, because I composed this myself; this wasn't... this is in the *Druid's Handbook* portion of *Merlyn's Complete Book of Druidism*—and this isn't actually taken from anywhere. It's something I composed to effectively systematize "Druid Ritual Tech" for, originally, a book called *Applied Druidology*.

In the Earth Phase, you're dealing with, you know, the "physical," the preparations, grounding, the "physical" aspects of the "Circle." In the Water Phase, you're dealing with the "internal set" and focus of the individual that is trying to change their own vibrations to meet that which they wish to attract.

"Druid Ritual Tech"—most Grade-I "magick" is based on the "sympathetic" aspect that "like attracts like." ...Because that's what's been observed with these traditions, so... [*Laughs*] The Air Phase, you're talking about "communication" again; you're talking about anything... sense, sound, smell, what's carried through the air. And then the Fire Phase, you're dealing with raising personal energy and incorporating energies and sending it to the goal.

These are elements of *any* ritual magic, but they particularly apply quite well to Druidry because traditionally Druidry, for example, like connected with the energies of trees, reading the signs and omens of Nature and things of that nature, it doesn't have the same kind of traditional sense of the "wizardcraft" or the mystical and magical elements that you might find in just traditional "ritual magic."

You don't see a lot of (quote; unquote) "Druid Spells," because, again, very little if anything of the "magickal lore" has really survived. The most that's survived on a literary level—a lot of it is the types of stuff we've already discussed (today) in terms of the "Triads" and the "Philosophies" and the "Doctrines" and what not. Those are all elements that we *can* actually draw from the relay of history and how things have kind of fallen down to us—but in terms of the actual practices; in terms of the actual verbatim "ritual grimoires" and things of that nature, we've kind of had to compose *that* ourselves, based on what we know of other traditions that were similar or around at the time; other sources; and then also the Bardic Verses.

There are really no incantations or specific verbiage attached to "Druid Magic"—the best that we've been able to derive, which I've excerpted a lot of—the best of—for the "Book of Pheryllt" or "Pheryllt Research" material contained in *Merlyn's Complete Book of Druidism.** These are the verses and poetry and elemental musings of the Bards and Learned Ones—and this is about as close as we have to any kind of incantations or anything.

Another point you'll find—and it's in there in the *Pheryllt Researches*—is the "Stanzas of the Graves." So, here would be another example of Douglas Monroe presenting what was considered the "Godform Evocation" or at the very least, the "Evocation of the Shade" of Merlyn. The concept that these Druids had such powerful personalities that they could basically become timeless; that they could... these storehouses of knowledge and experience would be able to be tapped later, in the form of "Shades"—kind of like "spirits."

---

* Now compiled in *"Draconomicon Vol. 2: The Pheryllt Researches."*

He composed an example of what something like that would be within the Druid Tradition. And it was kind of like— where did this even come from; what sense does it make... a lot of people were confused. Then we ended up discovering —when I was doing (personal) research for the Pheryllt tradition, because I had seen it written in Welsh, but then some translation notes on it—it was the "Stanzas of the Graves." The actual epitaph written on a gravestone at the supposed site of Merlyn, and this was actually employed in *The 21 Lessons of Merlyn* as the "Evocation."

And so this actually started to make more sense—there is more connectivity between how someone might reconstruct a modern Druid tradition based on the remnants and things that we *do* have access to and can actually have some kind of reality on. And this is something that's considered kind of innovative. It's something we have encouraged in the past decade with the development of *our* work underground, but it's something that is traditionally seen out there in the mainstream.

That's another reason why I've always found that the Monroe works were really an incredibly fascinating presentation —to be able to bring this kind of *real* aura of Druidry to life, whereas honestly most other perspectives, takes on it, presentations, they've really just kind of crossed a lot of "Celtic" concepts with that which is, for example, Route-A material—where for example, a lot of stuff that would be considered, well isn't considered, well it *is* considered, by the common [*laughs*] "New Age" masses—you know, it could be considered "Druidry" when it really is, for example, "Celtic Wicca." The presentation of basic Gardnerian or Alexandrian Wicca that just incorporates "Celtic Mythology" or a lot of Celtic legends or Celtic semantics in the observation of holidays and so forth.

I mean, this doesn't, of course, *make* it "Druidism." It makes it "Celtic Magic," which the two have been, I would say in the last twenty-five or thirty years of the rise of the "New

Age" materials out there—the two get easily confused with one another.

But you can educate your Seeker on the elements of "Ritual Tech" in the Druid Tradition—nothing wrong with that. They're there. They're in "Druid School" or their taking a "Druid Class," studying the elements... It's "magick." These guys are "magicians," right? They want to be able to *do* something with it. So, you take them through, you know, the "Elemental Tech"—the magical elements—you take them through the philosophies; take them through the basic principles of Druidism.

Although we are kind of shifting the curriculum or outline around a little bit to push the history—to combine the history with the history of Mesopotamia, since it correlates and this way to kind of be more concise for the purposes of our, the structure of our Master Course here... you'd want to present that too. Some kind of historical context; giving the reality on something before taking them down any kind of pathways in terms of philosophy or something. Give them the basics on history of whatever subject—whatever part of a course you're giving—so that it's something that can be referenced; there's something that can be looked up, or "Hey, you know, I think I saw something on the *'History Channel'* about that" or whatever it ends up being.

You take them through the "Phases" of "Ritual Tech" in the Druid Tradition. You start off again—we're doing the Earth-Water-Air-Fire sequence, as we talked about (yesterday). And we begin with personal preparations. That's preparing the Self, physically. In traditional magick, we're also talking about—you'll see in grimoires, in various preparatory information, or primers—about cleansing the body, scrubbing even. You'll see in some of the Hermetic texts: they talk about scrubbing the body to be able to get it to be able to breathe, take in more oxygen better.

You use freshly laundered linens. There is particularly a regimen where magicians are wearing robes and cloaks and specific attire for specific occasions. It's not only for energetic purposes, but the attending to, basically, "living deliberately"—making all the *acts*, being intentional, *deliberate*, and carrying them out with full Awareness.

That's one of the practices of "ritual magic"—when we talking about traversing the grades here and going back to what's worthwhile—you're doing "objective processing" (for those of you familiar with Grade-III Systemology), you're doing "objective processing" when you're doing "ritual magic."

You're commanding—maintaining some kind of control—the command of communication *between* the Mind-Body connection by deliberately telling the body to conduct these things, because of course, the individual, *You*, the individual is not their body—and we're getting into the habit of breaking some kind of automatic "mode" and doing a deliberate ritual act. So, these are all elements to be considered—also the preparation of the "Ritual Circle" itself; these would be part of the Earth Phase.

You'll see—books on spells and other practices and traditions—you know, "Don't break the Circle," and make sure you "Do this" and "Do that" and "Everything in the Circle." Well—just to maintain the focus of attention and the fact that you are *doing* something and being deliberate about it, yeah, you want to consider all the elements and all the tools and everything that you're going to be using—if such exists—to have them present.

There's also the tradition—it's, you know, carried over sometimes in the symbolism of witchcraft—but there's the tradition of "sweeping out" the area; cleansing the area of the location that you're going to practice the actual "ritual" or arrange your "Ritual Circle." Because, of course, you're treating it as a "space"—you're going to be creating "space" and "anchor points" in "space" to create a Circle and visualize that which you're wanting to attract within this microcosm—or within this personal universe that is being created.

And you also—in some traditions—you know, there's incense and smudge sticks and... virtually every tradition has its own methodology of "clearing" and "grounding" and "neutralizing" the existing energies both in the space and as far as an individual, you know—and that would be another facet of using particular garments or regalia that doesn't carry a lot of the static energy of going about in the world or the attention energies of other individuals when someone is going about their everyday life.

That—more or less—I mean, some sort of "Circle Casting" in that respect would be what you would be dealing with during the Earth Phase; the actual preparations of the Self, the Circle, and getting ready to do some "magick."

Now then, the Water Phase, the individual is supposed to be basically opening up channels and circuits and flows that are a point of connectivity between whatever they are treating as the "physical material universe" and the "mundane" and that which is their "personal universe"—which is, of course, a connection with Alpha-existence or "Spiritual Universe" or in a substitution of that, what people are sometimes treating as the "Astral Plane."

There's kind of this concept that, again, "something magical is going to happen." And so you're alerting consciousness to that, creating space, and designating it with a sense of purpose as to what is going to happen. And one of the ways which—in Elemental Magic or in Elemental Rituals or rituals based on the "Four Quarters" or you know, going to each of the directions and what not—you'll see, just kind of, a physical representation of setting up "anchor points."

So, whether you're setting up a Tablet to represent—you can use the "Signs of Portal" from your textbooks there—or some other "Elemental Tablet" or you're setting a candle of an appropriate color in that direction; you're basically putting out "anchor points" that are going to define the boundaries of the Circle, which is defining the boundaries of "space" that are treated as a "personal universe." Everything being basically connected to something else, via, either "thought" or some kind of mystical (Zu) energy or whatnot behind "sympathetic magic" being that things have an entangled quality to all other things and that they can be kind of influenced, then, at a distance.

In the Air Phase, you're dealing with the Mind, you're dealing with Thought—you're dealing [*laughs*] with Systemology. Well, what you're gonna do is—you want to basically begin with anything that is attached to the mental imagery; you basically have to process out, what we'd be doing with processing on any facet or anything that was giving someone an issue or that they're trying to resolve—you're basically trying to do that in ritual.

You're trying to basically "process out" any of the *attachments* or "negative associations" or *compulsions* toward or *compulsions* against—anything that involves whatever you're handling, whatever that might be, I mean this could be something to improve someone's attitude at work; this could be something to help someone be more *Aware* in their studies... I mean any of those "spellcraft" applications that you might find in grimoires or spellbooks or Wicca or whatever—whatever the intention is; whatever an individual is trying to attract into their life.

It's really better to work on the "attractive" than the "repulsive"—it's better to attract the things *in* that you want, rather than any kind of energy given to any kind of energy you're trying to keep away or push against. All that does is make a thing more solid.

The condition that you're trying to undo, it becomes more solid—because of the "intention-counter-intention" on the creation of it and the responsibility of it. So, the best thing you can do is simply *change* something; *override* something; *overwrite* something.

That's how you actually *undo* a lot of the "postulates" and "programming" at higher level Systemology that are encountered in an individual. You're simply outdoing them. You're not trying to "erase" them; you're not trying to sit there and "fight" against them; you're replacing them with a higher-level or a higher-powered, super-powered, thought that says, "Well, this other one is ridiculous." It's just not part of the reality anymore and therefore given no more energy.

A lot of times, when a person is trying to *change* when it comes to ritual magic and why ritual magic is not as effective as it *could be* applied, which you can *change* with a Master-level understanding—but they simply have too much of an energetic "charge" or "mass" or "store" or "tendency" attached to whatever the condition is that they're trying to change; which of course, inhibits the ability to properly *change* it!

So, you're working that all out at the Air Phase, *before* you're actually employing any actual energies or efforts or attentions *to* the change itself. A lot of that too would be also making sure you have a clear visualization of it. And this then leads right directly into the Fire Phase, which is basically working with the energetic flows of *that* visualization.

In this respect, we're talking about actually putting some kind of "charge" onto something—but, *not an emotional charge*. We're giving it a charge of attention; a charge of attention; we're giving it a push—and *never* a "pull." We're never trying to pull anything into us.

An individual is already sitting at an Awareness-Point at some point—usually not at Alpha—the average Seeker is going to be sitting at some Awareness-Point, basically suspended in place with a lot of mental imagery and pictures and scenes and energetic charges around them, and *these* are what they are fighting against usually when you are dealing with "low-level magick" or "spellcraft" or why people are endeavoring to use this to change their life. Whatever it might be—whatever Self-Help practice or regimen it might be.

It's the way in which the energy is handled and the way in which visualization and mental imagery is either maintained as either under control or not—that's going to entirely determine the effectiveness of it. The resolution in "ritual" is to basically see the change as taken place—to see it as a reality taking place—but not necessarily have any actual energetic or emotional charge *on* that.

A person "demanding"—you know, making demands of the universe—a person "pushing" too hard on the Universe is not going to... it's just going to find that it pushes back with an equal force and that the results are not optimum.

You want to basically have a fluid handling of mental imagery—which we've talked about previously with "magic"—and the ability to, you know, if you're actualized enough, the ability to actually stand in the point-of-view *outside* of the confines *of* the "physical body"—of the "genetic vehicle"—and actually push the imagery into the body; not pulling it down around us; not putting any actual force on it; but pushing it into the *body*, as a general thought.

One of the mistakes sometimes taking... when someone is applying any kind of ritual magic or basically Grade-I application of "magickal principles," is they've really confused "effort" and "Will." Rather than *willing* things into being, they are actually trying to duplicate the amount of *effort* it would take to actually physically do something or carry something out as with using the physical body. And of course, right now, we're dealing with the Mind-System; we're not dealing with trying to get the body over some kind of *somatic* troubles or some kind of *illness*, we are talking about maintaining control over the Mind-System.

That control is only really maintained in a kind of—certain clarity of Awareness. And this is a clarity of Awareness that —although it is obtainable, as I've demonstrated doing a preview of the Druidic work and the philosophies—whether or not an individual is going to just automatically *grasp* these realizations from their own casual exploration of these materials, usually remains to be seen.

That's one of the reasons for the Mardukite Master Course: to be able to go through all of these steps and whether or not they're necessary or of particular interest to every single Seeker or individual that is working up the *Pathway to Self-Honesty*—that there is a master-level understanding of them; that the knowledge and higher levels of realization accessible at the various levels *can* be gleaned by a master—such as yourselves—as being educated, on this quite prestigious course, to deliver that... to deliver that out to the world.

: LECTURE 17—THE ELVENOMICON :
(September 23, 2020)

[*This is Lecture-17 of the Mardukite Master Course—and we spent the first half of the day discussing elements of Druidism, your Druid School, Druid fundamentals, Druid philosophy, ritual tech involved in basic Druidism—and we might as well finish out the day, kind of focused in the same direction: Route-D of Grade-I. Now originally we were scheduled by the end of the day to have completed Grade-I. That's how it is originally scheduled for forty lectures. I believe we may end up extending the Mardukite Master Course, actually, to be forty-eight lectures. So, your schedule may be a little bit off there, but we'll get there—we'll get to where we're going and make sure we're covering everything that we necessarily need to cover in order to get this masterful understanding of the complete curriculum here.*]

So, this lecture will pertain to specifically the remainder of Route-D, which includes—we'll focus first and foremost on the materials of the *Elvenomicon*, which was originally developed as the *Book of Elven-Faerie*. As you know, *Book of Elven-Faerie* is one portion of what is now contained in the *Elvenomicon*.

It's not that I changed any of the material—as far as what's contained within, it's been revised—but, *Book of Elven-Faerie* was originally the title for one of three sections that was, that composed the anthology previously released as *Book of Elven-Faerie*. It was simply referred to that title—as that title—from the very beginnings.

I started putting it together in 2004 and released a version of it then. I spent a summer working on it and it didn't take very long to put together. Most of it was notes and material from my "Merlyn Stone" work and other Druidry research and work with the "Elven Fellowship Circle of Magick," most of which was never published in the *Sorcerer's Handbook* or any of those publications in the 90's.

So, after 2000, I started getting back into this work and the first of those works was "*Applied Druidology,*" which became *The Druid's Handbook*, and that just kind of got written and set on a shelf—I wasn't really working with any organizations in 2001, 2002, 2003... 2004. I was basically culminating and developing the work... just by myself, for myself, in kind of a preparation for unveiling this.

Because as you've seen, in the course of a very short period of time—you've seen a lot of these works come out, be reprinted, be referred to... ten, fifteen, twentieth anniversary editions. So, this was work that I was really just developing amongst myself and a few others that I was using as a "sounding-board" and some of my connections and underground networking that had been maintained from the 90's. But I wasn't really doing anything publicly.

It actually took five years—when I was working with a third-party publisher—it took five years from when I had set it, basically, released it from my hands in 2000, until 2005, for a publisher to do "*Merlyn's Magick,*" which is now out-of-print. It contained primarily *Sorcerer's Handbook* and a few other Druidic writings of mine from the "Merlyn Stone" period.

So, there wasn't a lot going on with me publicly visible at the time, but I was developing the material for *Elvenomicon*, and now it's "*Elvenomicon -or- Secret Traditions of the Elves and Faeries: The Book of Elven Magick and Druid Lore.*" And this is still the full materials as contained in *Merlyn's Complete Book of Druidism*, the Master Edition anthology for Route-D, contains all of this material.

When you start getting into this type of material—when you get into the concept of "Elves," "Faeries," even the "Dragon Legacy" and so forth—you are getting into material that, to understand it on any level beyond "mythological" or on a surface kind-of neopagan level, in terms of its applications, actually does require higher-level thought being applied to it.

Otherwise, this all seems very "fanciful." It all seems to be a little bit too "colorful," a little bit too "mythographic/mythological" in terms of what we hold true or what we consider about our physical universe—and so what we find here, in ancient times, as these traditions were developing, as they were the most prominent: we're talking about "mystical magical" traditions in the ancient world.

We're still referring to a time when human civilization as we understand it today is still being conceived of: cultivated and engineered into the way that we understand today—the parameters of that. You see a lot different cultures and a lot of different religious factions each imposing a certain set of guidelines or parameters for interpreting *reality*—and for that experience of reality.

This is something that you don't necessarily see as prominent up until about 2500 years ago. This becomes a standard. Now, in isolated situations—for example: Egypt or Mesopotamia or India or China or various factions of Europe or the Americas, certainly you have individual cultures and, what we consider, indigenous or primitive civilizations. Not "primitive" in their understanding but "primitive" in their "primary" origins of what was taking place with peoples as they were still primarily separated and developing individual.

Later you see widespread empires and huge religious crusades imposing specific cultural ideals or parameters of thought that become—that are just sweeping waves across continents—that begin to have an effect on the way in which all reality is later perceived thereafter... among even the common person that is basically instilled with a certain social organizational understanding of what *is* and what *isn't*; what *is real* and what *isn't*.

And we kind of begin to enforce this very stringently to *children*, when as very young adults, about: "This is real; that's not real; that's not possible" and so forth. Now, that's not to say that we have, you know, that there aren't better ways of handling this and other ways of processing different things and what's been carried with people—but we're talking about, on a global scale and on a large social scale, the beliefs basically impinging on what is considered *real* and *not real*.

A lot of the "imagery" that is attached to this—when we speak about "Elves" or "Faerie" or "Dragons"—it's not "one-to-one" necessarily with what will be immediately conjured to mind in the average person; and in that case, manipulates what is considered real—what is their experience or what is a tangible ledge of knowing or a reality to face on these matters, because an individual, of course, looking at this stuff and carrying into it a specific belief.

Either that, for example, a "being" that's been given an ancient classification, such as "Faerie" or "Dragon-race" and so on and so forth; either it's real or it's not real, or perhaps it's been demonized—you see this very commonly throughout the Middle Ages with the Christianization basically taking place throughout not only Europe but other areas as well. You see a lot of the iconic imagery and beliefs and representations of that which came before—particularly of the "pagan" people and ancient mythologies and such—being "demonized."

Basically having "screens" put up so that individuals won't confront them; won't look at them; won't see them for anything because, well, there's this "inherent danger that if you look into these things, well, you're gonna get taken over by the devil" or something of that nature. These things that were imposed on people for hundreds—and now almost thousands—of years, really has shaped what is considered *real*, what is *possible*, what is able to be beheld as reality.

So, a lot of these facets—in terms of underground factions of knowledge that have spread for thousands of years, isolated races and beings that were separate from what was taking place throughout the remainder of the "known world" or who was writing history at the time—we've only recently been going back to even look at these elements, because in the past they were hardly even conceivable.

The concepts of all of this, even within the Celtic and Druid paradigm, are always expressed within the semantics of that paradigm—what at one level, in ancient Mesopotamia or in the classical world, become "gods" or deities or later "demigods" or hybrids; we end up finding them turned into "angels" and "demons" based on various factions of religious mythology; "elves," "spirits," "pixies," each given later cultural connotations that really had very little to do—for example, the *pixie*, the "*pict-shee*," the Pictish "tribe," you know, they would actually paint, like henna-like tattoos all over, tribal-like tattoos, all over their face and what not. So, they were the "painted ones," the "*pict-shees*," and so you get this word "pixie." And then of course, you ask someone, "What's a Pixie?" And... "Oh, well, isn't that Tinker Bell, or something..."

So... obviously a change in how we have perceived what this terminology means over the course of thousands of years and this is something that is explored... *That* element *is* explored in the "Elven work" in you "Master Edition" there and in my works at a Grade-I level—at least exploring the semantics and the history and the development on that level.

Now, understanding—of course, at a Master Course level—understanding this true nature of what's taking place from a higher level; from a Systemological level, even the Actualized Wizard Level—you're dealing with, basically, remnants of two things: remnants of the "Gate work" that was taking place in an even older ancient period where a lot of it stems from, in the Ancient Near East and so forth, ancient Mesopotamia; and you're dealing with transitions still happening on a wide level between *this* Universe and the Magical Universe or the "Magic Kingdom" that we allude to a little bit in the Master Course—in these lectures—it's really not discussed at all until you start getting to Grade-IV technically, in the advanced courses and the "Wizard Level/Grades" of Systemology; but that *is* what we're dealing with here and it's something that we can express at least openly to *you*.

It's up to you to gauge and wherever your Seeker is at. We've divided these Grades for a reason to where this can be treated wholly and encompassing as a system of traditional Druidism or "ritual magic" and lore and work with "natural philosophy" and trees and elements and such—and then again, there is this "higher" Systemological advanced perspective that, at this level and the delivery in this course, we just simply don't dismiss it anymore.

We're dealing with transitions between the two Universes—back and forth between those that are still aware enough to make this happen, or as in other cases, once many were kind of pushed down and accepted the consideration that this particular *version* of beta-existence *was* the place to *be*. They started maintaining more of their lifetimes still in this local system—whether on this planet or another one—still in the Physical Universe, but this *other* Universe, again, that a lot of this descended from, you have elements of this "mystical" and "magical" existence being revived and carried.

And those that still carried this "memory" openly, that were still able to access it, (were) banding together and these become these kind of "figures" that stand out in the ancient world—those that the... "elves" and original "Druids" and then some of these other figures, which later were incorporated into the mythology. I mean these same figures from Celtic Mythology were originally exactly what I'm describing and you see these—there are hundreds of names in Celtic Mythology.

See, by the time of the "Celts"—you go from this, you know, in the more ancient part, the Celestial tradition, where it's really considered with more the greater Cosmos and the Star-Gates and so forth. Now once you get to the point of the European traditions and Druidism and the ancient Celts, you're dealing more with the Earth Deities and the "Earth Mysteries" and "Earth Mysticism" and Nature, as it pertains to the planet Earth in the physical world. Because that is *one* element that was still present in the Magical Universe.

In the Magical Universe things were a little bit more fluid, but they were still, for the most part, many of the same principles and the law... There was still a certain gravity to it and, you know, still certain conditions to it on a material level that are very similar to, for example, *this* Earth—when you take out a lot of the "electronics" and "space age" stuff.

The reason *why* you see, you know, prior to this kind of "mechanization" and "industrialization" of the world, you *see more* of these elements in place, because it was more prominent in the minds of these individuals—these higher minds that were still able to carry a lot of this information through. And so there *is* a time where, at least according to the Druidic lore and the Faerie lore, that there were at least a more accessible knowledge concerning access to "Gates" or "portals" or "thresholds" or things of that nature [*right*] that connected these two Universes where this was still a known "technology."

So this is one of those things that you really only see shadows and allusions to and—the concepts of—later thereafter in all of the magical lore, you never see it really getting back to that as a main point; it's mostly about how to get along better in *this* world as time goes on. And so even though they still refer this "ancestral memory" and they do all these "ritual acts" in commemoration to this legacy that brought it here, the actual "access" to the "technology," you know, beings being here physically and then suddenly not—this isn't what we see taking place anymore.

We see the ability to at least, at the very least, shift our point-of-view; that our point-of-view has been fixed into, for example, using *this* physical body, and when we release our point-of-view of that, we are able to access other planes, other existences at least at a mental level. But, unfortunately when it's restricted to the "Astral work" of the "New Age" movement of the last, let's say, hundred-and-fifty years—this is still very much connected to the "Mental Plane." It isn't necessarily getting somebody back to a "spiritual" existence or Actualized *as* the Spirit *as* Self operating *as* the Alpha Spirit.

Most of the time, "Astral work" is still very much concerned with carrying around a lot of the "identity" and "personality" and "mental imagery"—an individual is seldom totally free of that as a fragmentation, when delving into some of the more "mystical" and "magical" presentations of treating, for example, "Astral work" and so forth. It's not to invalidate what's taking place there, but again, we're looking at a higher understanding of these elements and facets of, for example, Grade-I traditions when we treat it at the Master Course level, in that we know there are certain effective elements of them; that each of these traditions will be found effective within their own paradigm, mainly because they hit on—sometimes very randomly—a point of actual truth and a point of effectiveness.

And so, what we've actually done with Systemology—in bringing these up to the Master Grade and the Wizard Levels—is looking for those points of effectiveness. Taking those points that are actually effective, that are making any of these other systems useful, and basically peeling away the rest; that a lot of the extra semantics and cultural jargon and so forth are unnecessary to the elements that are actually effective within them.

But, of course, what we do with your "Magic School" or your "Wizard School" or your "Druid School" or even creating an "Elven-" or "Otherkin-" Society as some have done these days, is your able to explore some of these facets *within* a paradigm that can be grasped. So, we treat it as "Celtic Druidism" or "Elven-" or the "Dragon-" tradition, due to how it's been presented to us; the tradition in which we are exploring it as—being Western Europe, and that which it's represented and the iconic imagery.

But as we saw with the "Druid Philosophies" and some of the other fundamentals, the points of fact and the points that are actually effectively useful as you move up through the Grades are not restricted to simply participating in strictly a tradition that would be "Druidism" or "Neopaganism" or anything—any kind of strict adherence to a specific flavor or tradition.

These elements are just there as demonstration points, which gives you something colorful and tangible in your classes and working with Seekers, to give them something to work with and actually like *hold* tangibly—to be able to dress up, participate, to have an understanding of the medias and the fantasy stories and be able to relate it something; so long as, again, when we deal with this as a Master Course, we don't want anyone to get too restricted to one paradigm or another to where that ends up being the end-all be-all, and to which any higher level or gradient remains out of reach.

Because the only way that they could understand anything would be, for example in this sense, the Elven-Faerie or Druidic paradigm. So, we're trying to make sure that while we're exploring all these things, we're getting kind of this grand tour of 6000 years of *esoterica* and what it actually is and just "calling 'spades' for 'spades'," we also don't want [*laughs*] anyone getting too enamored with the "flashing lights" and the distractions along the way, because we've found...

Back in 2005, I would have probably been very (predominantly) developing a kind of "Elven Quasi-Anunnaki Tradition" that is purely in a "Druidic" or kind of "Renaissance Festival" styling, until I was really able to spend the time to work further. And again, in Grade-II we end up beyond Europe and straight into Mesopotamia. And in the next lecture, we'll start to get into where the parallels on that is —and *why* this became such a matter of significance, in terms of Mesopotamia and Druidism, because most to this day *still* are not really—they don't really have a reality on any real connection there.

The whole purpose of this *is* to, again, to incorporate a "Druid School" as part of, basically what we were describing a couple days ago, the *flattening*, or just the "calling it *is* what it *is*" and seeing things as they are so that we can handle them, confront them, face them, and move along the *Pathway*. Otherwise a lot of this stuff becomes a "Mystery." I mean, this tradition, especially in ancient Europe and so forth, this is very "mysterious mystical magical" stuff—and it's been... people have, much like any other facet of the occult, there have been many that have dedicated entire lifetimes to the exploration of this paradigm and just this semantic-set.

Within this portion of the Mardukite Master Course, we are treating the Western European Tradition—the European Tradition in general—the migration from the Ancient Near East to where we things today as it basically maintained its last remnants of survival, for example, in the British Isles, Scotland and Ireland and so forth; and then of course, it being carried *into* the Americas.

So this has been a *long* migration over thousands of years and of which is very rarely untouched or virgin, because it has had *many* hands on it—it has had many traditions, many biases, many opinions—before it's reached the state that it is today.

One of the commonalities of those that have been drawn to the "Elven Way" and the "Celtic Faerie Tradition" and even those that have assumed the same, just under the guise of "straight" Druidry—since this other... the idea of a modern "Elven Tradition" "Faerie Tradition" as we're presenting it, is "Druidic," is a semantic that is still only up and coming. But what it is, we're dealing with—I mentioned "Otherkin Festivals" and those that band together with this—we're talking about those that have, kind of, tapped that multi-level understanding of it; those that are Aware that *they are* in fact—they as individuals—not restricted to the Human Condition.

Now this is one of the things that we're "gradiently" [*laughs*] working someone up on the *Pathway to Self-Honesty* and freeing their considerations and then developing, in Systemology for example, you know, the "I-AM" or the "Alpha-Spirit" independent of *any* "body" or "considerations" or "personalities" or anything that might be developed thereafter—or assumed as a "point-of-view."

What we find interesting here with the Elven Tradition and the Faerie Way and all of this, is that we *have* individuals that are very much aware—and this includes actually the "Dragon races" and even into "vampyrism"—we are talking about: not people that are necessarily deluded because they, "Oh, well, they're running around and they look like you and me and da-da-la-da."

Okay, because, you see, that again is one of those "misnomers"; restricting what it means to be "elf" or "fae" or of the "dragonkind" or of a "vampyric descent" to *some* kind of "Hollywoodized" or "Disney Version" or *some other* iconic imagery that's been, kind of, put "up" for us to kind of almost show how ridiculous something like that might be; or just to kind of like give it this *mask*, so: "Oh... you know [*laughs*] it's just *that*."

So, really, at the end of the day you've got individuals that, pure and simple, are realizing that the condition of "Self" is *not* restricted to the Human Condition. So... That's just one element of looking at these traditions and so, that's also one element that has separated, for example, the Grade-I Route-A presentation—which is, you know, like *Sorcerer's Handbook* and such, as a very straightforward, very contemporary, kind of a commonality or standard of what is acceptable as the "New Age" material within the "New Age"—and then as I worked toward the *Elvenomicon* and the aspects of *Arcanum*, (I) was leading towards these realizations that, for me, wasn't so much of a realization as me realizing ways that I could *relay* information to others; ways that others would be able to understand; ways that I could communicate.

Within Route-D, we're primarily dealing with these elements that are actually a step *beyond*—a step *between*—the traditional Route-A *Arcanum* style of general magic, practical magic, ritual magic, magickal traditions and orders, the kind of stuff that you'll just find in your local bookstore—versus the *deeper* traditions and the origins of the Western Magical Tradition and just how deep that really does go, and how far an individual is actually willing to go with that.

Where Druidism is concerned, the origins really do lie within this secret tradition of "Elves" and "Faerie" and "Dragonkind" and all of this stuff that really does go back to an even more ancient world than is reflected within the "Celtic tradition" or the Western Magical Tradition verbatim—something that predates even that.

Obviously before we get into *those* elements—which would be primarily Grade-II—we wrap up Grade-I with Route-D, which is of course, the "Route of Druidism and the Dragon Legacy."

As I was explaining earlier (today), this methodology is specific to the paradigm and semantics of the Western Europe or European Tradition or Celtic Druid Tradition—or what we'll get into as the "Danubian Druid Tradition"—but it's all encompassed within *Merlyn's Complete Book of Druidism* as the Master Edition for this route. And within this Route, we're basically dealing with a direct bridge—it isn't just bridging one or another facet or trying to show parallels—we're dealing with a direct bridge to the Grade-II material and dealing with Mesopotamia and the ancient origins prior to its migration through Europe.

[*So, the rest of the day, we'll focus specifically on the European aspects and the way in which it's been relayed in terms of the "Elven Tradition," the "Faerie Tradition," the "Dragon Tradition" and we'll make sure to get some of that practical tech in there too, as a way of relating to your "Magic Schools" and such—and we should have a good time of it.*]

: LECTURE 18—DANUBIAN DRUIDISM :
(September 23, 2020)

[*Editor's Note: This transcript begins with the lecture already in progress, as did the original recording.*]

Although in the ancient Celestial, Mythological and Pantheistic systems that were derived from specifically the "planets," those traditions such as in Mesopotamia are observed in a more—more of a "priestly" practice; more religious connotations attached really to specific deities.

Now, when you look at either end of this—whether you move to the East or you move to the West—you see more of an emphasis on the "elementalism," and the "elemental" patterns. And a lot of that, in the Celtic tradition or in the Western tradition, a lot of the associations of that are attached to the origins—as they document it—of Druidism. Specifically "Danubian"—or "*Danu*-bian" Druidism. And this would be those primarily connected to what you've see as the "*Tuatha D'Anu*."

And *that* is a nomenclature that *I actually* developed—it's ironic to see it now being used elsewhere in... to connect the "Ancient Druids" with the "Anunnaki"—but that was something I actually developed specifically in my works. And it was not treated very popularly.

Unfortunately there's still many that cling on to very specific semantic paradigm viewpoints in regards to these studies —these mystical studies, which are supposed to be opening up one's considerations and freeing one's individual to conceive and perceive of [*laughs*] all these different things. And yet what we find—and this is why, as a Master and when we're guiding Seekers through this material, we want to be able to show the parallels in that we are referring to specific semantics when we deal with this. And most of the time their not even correct; they're just ways we have to group knowledge and associate knowledge.

Most of the semantics that we carry, even to the present day, in regards to ancient history, really pertains to the way it was documented by some of the classical writers—primarily like the Greeks—as opposed to the way we might understand it from the point-of-view of these individual cultures themselves.

Even the word "Druid" and "Celt" comes from Greek writings; Greek identifications of their encounters with the British priesthoods—what we refer to as the "Druid" and the "Celt." There *is* a Welsh term: "Derwydd" [*der-with*]— which is spelled D-E-R-W-Y-D-D, so you could say "*der-widd*" or "*dru-id*" if you want to put it that way...

So, in that respect—in seeing that—the Greeks eventually classified the entire Order and System and College and classification of these as the "Druids" completely, and that was something done in Greek writings and of which we use today as our classical sources for understanding Druidism.

But, of course, in ancient times, you know, 2500 years ago, the Druids themselves, did not necessarily refer to even the body of their Order as the Druid Order or so forth—these are ways that others have later come to understand it and then classify it; the same with Mesopotamia.

Mesopotamia was never referred to as "Mesopotamia" by the ancient *Mesopotamians*, that's again, a Greek classification of the region, meaning "Land between two rivers" in the *Greek* language; not in any Sumerian language. And then, even the concept of "Sumerians" or the "Land of Sumer"—there *was* a land of Sumer and Akkad... the Sumerians never actually referred to *themselves as* "Sumerians." You see? This is something that's later done by others.

In the Sumerian language there is no word for "Sumerian." Okay? In terms of the language or in terms of the culture or the land it's always referred to as like... for example, the Sumerian... the "language" is always written *in* Sumerian as, like, "mother tongue." Or... and then, the land: "mother land" and things of that nature—it's not classified in the way that *others* later accounting for it, or referring to it, from the *outside*, are classifying.

It is *always* these *outside* perspectives that are primarily explored in the pursuit of conventional history. Which is why we deal with "esoteric archaeology" or "alternate history" and then there's some people that use the word "forbidden" although no one is really out there "forbidding" any of this...

It's just that *this* is not the "common everyday man's" version of history—of which has mainly been spoon-fed by those that are really in no better position to define describe it as the next person. But it's become the common denominator of understanding—the common knowledge—which this Game maintains; the information that we assume that all the "players" are basically aware of, this common knowledge is really some of the lowest-level information or "postulates" to base a Life and Reality on as you could get.

Really looking any deeper that, it requires those that are willing to actually take that step and actually face or look up to these facets of society for what they actually are—and not just for the way they've been presented in the past.

As the traditionally story goes: the *Tuatha d'Anu*—or "Children of the Stars" is really what it represents when you look at the semantics behind who the beings are and tracing vocabulary (which is one of the ways I was able to, kinda, track the tradition across Europe)—you see references to the beings pop up as either the "White Folk" or the "Shinning Folk" or the "Light Beings" or "Star Beings" and you see this appear throughout a lot of different indigenous mythologies and in the lore behind a lot of different "mysticism" that relates to "ancestral deities" or any of the "Faerie"-type elementals or any of this type of thing.

Clearly these "Children of the Stars," they arrived in Keltia —which is what we refer to as all of the "Druidic" lands or "Celtic" lands in the materials and the Master (Course) materials—and they arrived on Beltane, which is May's Eve. And so we see an emphasis here on a specific point: and this is the origins, of course, of the Celtic observation of May's Eve.

Now, there's other aspects to observing this tradition today —such as those that follow "Great Bear" (constellation) circle around and different ways of plotting magical timing and calendars—but the significance of Beltane, being the "Fires of Bel" is what that name means in Celtic language, is that they arrived and apparently (as the story goes) the air was in enshrouded in smoke for almost three days from them burning their "ships."

They basically burned their "ships"—whatever they arrived in—just burned them to cinders. This, of course, has begged the question to some: "is that like a *crash landing* of some kind?" or "did they just straight up burn the ships?—some kind of sea-faring ships..." But the references in lore, of course, just saying "ships," and then, of course, them being "burned to cinders"—there's obviously no traces or evidence of them [*laughs*] thereafter.

And when you're dealing with The Book of Elven Faerie [*Elvenomicon*] you'll also find references to the "*Sylva d'Terrestai*"—or the "*Book of the Everlasting Forest*," I think it's called—which is really a version, as far as I could tell, and this is something I was exploring a couple decades ago for an org... a group that was trying to treat this Elven Tradition a little bit more seriously; this is before there really was a lot of presence for such "Elven-Faerie-Otherkin" traditions—or the internet groups and so on and so forth.

So far as I could tell, it's a human [Elven] version of the *Urantia Book*, which unless you're going to get into all that semantics and go tracing down *that* path, there's really no reason to get too involved with it other than it presents—if you're looking at the Elven semantics or specifically excluding any knowledge of even the other route of Grade-I or anything that comes after it, or chronologically before it since we are referring to ancient Mesopotamia in Grade-II—it's simply a version of, for example, the "Anunnaki Genesis" and the involvement from just a different semantic-set.

Most of this ancient lore—when you spend enough time, as I have, digging through all the piles of it and each tradition's version of these things in their own language—I've across most of it, basically, talking about the same stuff, but talking about it as if you did have a member of a different language and a different background and a different viewpoint and different personality programming... Each person basically explaining or interpreting these basic events.

So when you start to boil them all down and you peel back some of the cultural semantics and the beliefs about various titles and names that these things have been given, you start to see the commonality much more—and this is where you start to acquire that wide-angle view.

So, when the "Danubians" arrived in the Celtic lands—they arrived in Ireland actually. And they discover that it was already actually inhabited by a different, basically, Elven-Faerie race—descendents of... called "Nemed" or "Fir Bolg," which basically just means "Men of Bags"—but the Fir-Bolg, as it explains in the *Book of Invasions*, which is an Irish manuscript, they were forced to take shelter as a result of the smoke and the fog and everything... They weren't really sure what had actually taken place when the Danubians arrived and basically treated the... as an invasion—a hostile invasion—as recorded in this Irish manuscript called the *Book of Invasions*.

And so you actually have a "war" ensue between these two "Faerie" races in ancient times—and we... I... It's probably not what we would consider "war" today, in terms of the type of activities taking place, but yeah—the fact that there was already preexisting, you know, preexisting society taking place in the "Celtic" lands as the Danubians, kind of, moved through and, kind of, set themselves up as the "higher minds" amidst them.

And so you start to see a lot of the associations—very specific—to "Elemental Magick." Those arrive in, specifically, in relation to the lore that's presented in, for example, the *Book of Invasions*, because each of the elements is ascribed these like, for example, Earth is given "North" and Air is given "East" and we find many reasons why we can *qualify* this to be the case—we've discussed that (a couple days ago) in regards to Elementalism—but when we're dealing with Druidism specifically and Druidic lore, it refers to the Danubian Druids being represented by *four* "Leaders," each coming from a different "Kingdom" in their own rights prior to their emigration to the Celtic lands, and each of them carrying with them a particular "Magical Artifact."

And it just so happens to correspond, for example, the "Cauldron," which is associated with "Water" and associated with the "Western" direction—would just so happen to be represented by a figure that was the King, you know, the King of the Western Kingdom, which carries the Cauldron—and then the King of the Southern Kingdom, representing Fire, carries the Sword of Nuada. And Lugh, from the Kingdom of Air, carries the Spear, which is like the equivalency of the Wand in the East. And then the sacred Stone, the Stone of Fal—the Sacred Stone, the Stone of Destiny—on which the Kings were later "crowned" in Ireland, came from a Northern Kingdom represented an Earth Guardian.

And so, you see these—they're referred to as the "Gifts of Faerie"—but then, you know, it's simply a matter of simple transference to see how an Air Spear from the East becomes the Wand in ceremonial magic and so forth. And there's even individuals today that have practiced—there's some works by a gentleman named Steve Blamires, and his works, he's described actually reenacting Irish Druidism using these tools. So, in the north you're setting out a huge stone; and you consecrate a large Spear of Lugh and place that in the East and so forth.

So the idea of apply ancient iconic imagery and symbols this way—the concept of applying them to the elements, using them as ritual correspondences and so forth—this is an ancient concept. Of course, we know the ideals of "Magick" and "mysticism"—the "Power of the Self"—and all that, is not restricted to or allocated to any or one ritual tool, but we see these tools, you know, take a presence *in* the tradition as it's finally solidified, in terms of "Celtic Druidism" and "Elven Way" and "Faerie Tradition" as a way of reenacting—or as a way of dramatizing—these various ritualistic and ceremonial applications.

So, I had someone pose a question about why I don't follow the curriculum outline described with the "Master Course" [in the "*Instructor's Manual*" and appendices to the Master Editions] and so I should answer that. Of course, we're trying to get through the material at an accelerated pace for you—and then of course, a lot of that curriculum outline stuff regards the way material is set up in a book.

Obviously books tend to be presented—given that an individual, like an author such as myself, can never really determine to what extent or what background an individual has a handle on things prior to reading a particular book and then what other books in association with that—and so the outline really is to go along with the materials because the common-ground here being that more individuals are going to be accessing this through the *books* rather than through the *audio*.

And that's why as "Instructors" or as "Masters" or however you're participating in this chain, it's really for *you* to be able to judge really what the best design of a curriculum outline is. I've simply provided a guideline to work it through it as it's chronologically given in each individual book and then blending that together, because we have quite a bit of material here in the "Master Course" for just the "Route of Druidry and the Dragon Legacy" that, as I said, you could develop an entire "Magic School" or "Wizard School" or "Druid School" specifically on those explorations alone and be dealing with that material for quite some time, depending on how far you take it.

In the outline for *Irish Book of Invasions*, I mean I have here that it "ascribes the origins of Danubian Druidism; that it's linked to the La Tene culture" which is the culture—it's actually described by historians (by) the way it designed its art and pottery styles and some of the ways in which the "spiral patterns" and, kind of, familiar "Celtic" designs can be traced back to the Ancient Near East, based on the use of it, by this "La Tene" culture.

And that's what kind of clued me in to—particularly the fact that one of the routes that had been taken was called "Danube River" and I thought that seems almost too simple, and as it turns out, yeah—it's for sure related to this tribal migration that was taking place.

How this tribal migration that we've been able to chart—in terms of the establishment of the Celtic culture and "Danubian Druidism"—and then the actual arrival of the *Tuatha d'Anu* in Ireland and the burning of ships and all that, are kind of two distinct things.

When you look at Ireland and Britain, the way in which the geography is set up, the Westerns—or the, yeah, well, Western Europe—but the European mainland actually lies to the east; you're traveling west from the mainland to get to those islands.

And as it is recorded, the Danubian Druids ended up showing up from the north and west, from the complete other direction, when they settled in Ireland. For whatever reasons that may be. And so there's a lot of conjecture open to that.

But the *Book of Invasions* also describes that there were multiple "racial" invasions of the Celtic lands in prehistoric times. And by "prehistoric," we mean prior to history being recorded. This really can apply—it's not a specific date—it really applies to at any point in culture where history is not yet being recorded in that culture.

I mean, ironically, even in—even after the invention of the mass-duplication of materials and so forth—the manuscripts that we refer to that are the basis of Druidism, like the Irish manuscripts here and so forth, I mean they are making accounts as though they are very ancient knowledge.

But even these are—all of the materials are less than 500 years old as source, written, materials—when it comes to Celtic tradition *in* Celtic writing. Prior to that, we don't really have much record because of the over-Christianization and other dogmas that really suppressed—ever since the Roman Empire—the ability to communicate the true "Celtic" tradition.

And even prior to that all of the libraries and storehouses of information and so forth were destroyed by the Romans to pretty much—I mean they spent 1000 years trying to eradicate any traces of Druidic tradition. And then they ended up —their Empire ended up falling themselves. [*Laughs.*] That's how that went down.

Multiple racial invasions—the *Nemedians*, which were the "Sons of the Sun"; the *Fomorians*, the "People of the Sea"; the *Fir-Bolg*, which here I have translated as "Men of the Dark Earth." And then finally, the "Children of Anu" or the

"Children of the Stars"—this emergence of a Danubian Druidism, which is about where things begin to pick up in terms of our understanding of Druidism: what Druidism represents; the Elements as I mentioned; the tools and so forth—granted they have their own lore attached to how these classifications and elemental correspondences have come together; but it's no less effective when we compare it to the other "Elemental" paradigms; they are all working within the same Elemental tradition under various languages.

A concise synthesis of this "backbone-fundamental-elemental"—the ritual concepts that were all devised from it—the fundamentals here really can be derived directly from these "*Gifts of Faerie.*" Even the elements of "Celtic Mythology" often overlap with these themes—and we see concepts of it all throughout global mythologies and certain commonalities here.

So, we have the *Stone of Fal*, from the Northern city of Falias, coming to us from Morfessa, the High Wizard of the North. This was set at *Tara*, the "Seat of the Kings," which is literally like the "Dragonkings of Ireland" and it would scream out whenever a true king had set foot on it. And the of course, with Irish Druid history, we are explained: only the Kings of Ireland in Celtic times were *made* there and crowned there on the Stone of Fal—only the true kings; kingship as an integral part of the "Dragon Legacy."

The esteem of leadership and sovereignty and what it represented was specifically tied to this legacy—and that there was a true element to it. We see the same thing with, kind of, our everyday knowledge of "Excalibur"—the whole "Sword in the Stone" (motif)—that it could only be released from the stone if the "True King" came along.

And *that* is actually even derived from, for example, the "*Sword of Nuada*" coming from the city of Finias, carried from the South by Uscias—according to this Mythology. And yeah, this is the archetypal "Magic Sword"—the Blade, "*Albion*," "*Caliburn*," "*Excalibur*" and what have you. Of course, it had the "magical" ability to basically deal a direct fatal blow with each strike. It was the sure certainty and cutting will—the searing edge of power—directed by the operator.

Thereafter we allocate, for example, the Sword or Blade as a symbol of Fire and the South, so there's another example. And the of course, we were discussing the *Spear of Lugh*, when I listed these—also known as the "Spear of Destiny." Ironically, all of these tools are also referred to as the "objects-of-destiny"; so—The Stone of Destiny; The Spear of Destiny; The Sword of Destiny... the concept of Destiny seems to run pretty parallel here—which we again approach pretty directly in Grade-III, especially with the entry-level *Liber-One: Tablets of Destiny*. [*Laughs*]

But the *Spear of Lugh*—according to the lore—emerge from the Eastern city of Gorias and it's carries by Estas. And it's the spear that essentially never missed its target—much as the *Sword (of Nuada)* could be wielded and it would be a critical hit [*laughs*] every time—this was a spear that would find its target. So it would be directed to a target and not miss; it would be able to, like with a *wand*, direct the flow or attention to the target—and of course became a symbol of the Element of Air and allocated to East and so forth, which again, we can represent with a *Wand.*

And then finally, the *Cauldron of Dagda*—it's also... in Celtic Mythology it reappears as "Kerridwen's Cauldron of Rebirth"—and that's directly related to Pheryllt lore and such —but the legends explain that it came to Ireland by Master Semias, which... who came from the city of Murias (from) the West.

In one of the legends the Cauldron acts as like a "Horn of Plenty"—it just keeps filling itself with an endless supply of food. And then there's another piece of lore that would suggest the artifact had a part in "healing rituals," where it could revive and cure the wounded—repair them—you know, you could stick your hand in and it would fix your hand. In later traditions—for example, in the "Arthurian Traditions"—which later emerged, kind of, out of British Welsh Druidism during the Celtic period, or during the Christian period (rather), by that time, the Cauldron and this "cauldron concept" is connected—via Christianity—with the "Holy Grail." The same kind of life-giving; the pursuit of the "Grail" as carrying the "Great Mystery" or the "Legacy."

There's other [*laughs*]—of course, in this day and age—there's other connections to the "Dragon Age [Legacy]," which is specifically connected to what you've actually found in some of the "alternative history" and "da Vinci Code"-type work—"Holy Blood, Holy Grail"—and so forth. You'll find that there's a "Grail Tradition" also, that emerges, in the Celtic lands, that's connected directly to Jesus, the Jesus bloodline, the Jesus legacy—in the m.. [*laughs*]

Ironically, the preservation of this legacy—in the midst of those that would necessarily, you know, yeah, they carry the "name," but basically used it to represent that was basically *opposite* to the teachings of Jesus himself. So... And a few of these things also... The Spear of Light—I mean, some references to a "Spear of Destiny" that you'll find, you'll find a connection to that too. The "Spear of Destiny" in *some* legends is actually the tool or implement to pierce Christ's side at the crucifixion and supposedly became thereafter this, you know, a significantly powerful artifact.

So you see... There's a common play here of different themes that you're going to find if you explore... I mean, I've focused on some of the more basic ones—and particularly the "Celtic" tradition—then we go into Mesopotamian tradition. But once you explore, for example, "Druidry" and "Mesopotamia" and this particular stream as it evolved into the Western Magical Tradition, it really doesn't matter from there—if you examine, for example, other forms of Western traditions or African traditions or Eastern traditions or other semantics, you will see the common... even the Egyptian and the Roman and the Greek phil... mythologies and so forth—you will begin to see these certain common parallels.

And these (mythological) figures: although each one is presented within their own point of view as, pretty much, the *epicenter* of all existence—or the known world—when you take a step back, you'll find that each one of these *epicenters* was actually correlating with all these *other* epicenters; and that they were actually all having, you know, very similar experiences with very similar "*beings*" that all had very similar, basically, background stories and so forth.

But each was relayed just a little bit different and specific to the language, the culture, the values, the ideals, the... geographies of different places. Certain mountain would be a home of the God—and if you went 3000 miles in a direction, you'd find another mountain, which was the home of the Gods and was the birthplace of whatever and if you, you know; each one had established their own version of this. And this is—it's not until really you start to see the mass migration of human populations that any of this was really... start to be able to be brought together under a *new* "Mystery School."

Unfortunately the populations—as ignorant as they were as they migrated—really just carried with them *their own* values, their own tradition, their own paradigms and then, you know, set out to interpret or invalidate whatever they were coming upon each step of the way.

But... now, at this point: we're here in the 21st century; we've got a Master-level understanding that we can access, in which to work with all this material; and we no longer have to be restricted to any one or another paradigm or semantic-set, when we set out to realize and discover what is *true*.

: LECTURE 19—FAERIE TRADITIONS :
(September 23, 2020)

The "Elven Histories" and the History of the Druidry and the Elven Way—the Faerie Faith as it evolved; as it developed—is relayed very succinctly in the *Book of Elven-Faerie* portion of the *Elvenomicon*, or in *Merlyn's Complete Book of Druidism* and it could be explored and relayed in a diversity of ways; it could be connected very easily to studies of the "Dragon Legacy" (as when we'll be talking about the *Draconomicon*); it also relates very clearly to the Mesopotamian pursuits.

There's no reason to get too deep into all the nitty-gritty details of history—for the purposes of *this* Master Course—that's something that's relayed very clearly; it doesn't [*laughs*] require a lot of explanation when you look over the materials.

However, the basis of it being—when you look at an examination of history and cultures and the "mystical" developments from the ancient times and then how it later evolved in the religions and traditions we carried through the Classical period—what you end up seeing; you see this with the Mesopotamian and Anunnaki; you see this with the presence of those same Celestial Deities when they are appearing in other cultures, whether it's the Greeks or the Egyptians; and you see this present even in the populations of the "Elven" and "Faerie" and "Dragonfolk" directly in terms of ancient history—and that is the *Rise of Humans*.

As you see a greater rise in the *Human* population, you see, basically, those that are preexisting in "power," kind of bowing out—and setting up other infrastructures and traditions.

Now, in the case of, for example, the Anunnaki in Mesopotamia—I mean this was kind of almost an "archetype" or a "blueprint prototype" area of development—so you see an institutional "class" step in, where you have "Priests" and ambassadors and a specific lineage of "Kings" that's all tied to the Anunnaki directly. There's considered a "bloodline" or a "legacy" or a specific "genealogy" that is carried forth; and you see "Kingship"—you see this in the concept of the "Dragon King," you see this in ancient China, all throughout ancient Mesopotamia, in the pharaonic dynasties of Egypt; you see this in any classification or use of "Dragon" iconic imagery to represent "Kingship" and "sovereignty" all throughout Europe.

And of course, this all goes back to a specific programmed association between the "Dragon," "The Land," the ordering of cosmic systems and the sovereignty of "Kingship." And so this symbolism gets laid out and we find these specific "beings," which at first are essentially "gods" when you look at the very root of it; the farthest back—the Anunnaki, the Celestial deities—these are considered gods."

And we don't mean as "God" with a capital "G" as the "Origin of All Things" and so on and so forth—but their status; their status in their relationship with the physical universe. And the status of the ruling power and its representation with the "Divine Right to Rule" is always a mirror of this— this higher idea. And so it's put in place—it was implanted— in the consciousness that in the absence of these "gods," then we would have specific "Priest-Kings" and a specific lineage of mystics and so forth, you know—might be half-breeds or quarter-breeds or hybrids or however you want to look at that—they were considered a separate class of being in relationship to the rest of the population.

Now, of course, in terms of "history" and in terms of the way we look at the physical sciences, a lot of this gets related back to—we're talking about—actual physical bloodlines. This of course, begs the question—and a lot of hooptyloo gets brought up about this on the internet, concerning RH-negative blood-types and all this stuff.

Really, what you want to look for behind it all is commonalities—what is being relayed here: it's a demonstration of various genetic manipulation down through the ages; it's the establishment of various traditions and "shadow traditions" and "underground traditions" carrying specific lineages, which would otherwise be lost, watered-down or diluted through the common population...

And so, these are all important aspects, but to... When we look at it from a systemological perspective, to consider, again, any of these aspects purely from the physical perspective is to be incredibly limiting about it. And therein being, the beautiful trapping [*laughs*]—since we've been putting this out along the way—the beautiful trapping of Route-D.

Because any concept that—a specific bloodline, a specific...—at this juncture; because of the widespread diversity of culture, the shifting populations around the globe, all of the diverse ways in which people have been educated, initiated and so forth—to limit anything to any one or another "genetic vehicle" type at this juncture, we know to be a falsehood. That would just only further contribute to fragmentation.

We know that these vehicles, as the Human Condition, are actually capable of an incredible amount, regardless of any of their ancestry. We also know that genetic memory can be easily resolved in an individual—as far as the separation of that identification with *Self*, because any of these beliefs that the Elven or Faerie races at this juncture, those that are occupying physical existences at present time, would require one or another specific vehicle to carry, is ridiculous.

We know that Alpha-Spirits are able to come in and out all the time. We know that beings from, you know, that have experienced not only countless lifetimes in *this* Physical Universe, but other universes as well, are able to come in and assume points-of-view and command and control over the physical condition of a "body."

It's only when a person is "entrapped" in that, that we start to get into trouble. It's only when the consideration of "Self" is *for and as* the "body," we start to get into trouble. And so when we refer to these various (quote; unquote) "Races" and types and so forth—yeah, of course, back in ancient times, there was definitely a significant difference between various populations and cultures and so forth; most of which were operating fairly remotely to one another, up until 2500 years ago.

For all the intents and purpose, I mean, 2500 years ago was about the time when the Greeks *first* encountered the Celtic people and the Druids—in terms of writing about them, giving any kind of history about them, about 500-600 B.C. And we have to assume that between then and now, there was *that much* time period taking place—if you consider the origins of Stonehenge and things of that nature—all of that time period taking place *before any* Classical encounters, or Greeks or Romans or anything to encounter to write about for the history that *we* still have today.

And so, anything prior to that in the "Celtic" lands is essentially "prehistory," because it becomes open to archaeological and anthropological consideration and speculation. We can carbon-date various sites all we want, or tried to. We can make comparison between certain styles of art and pottery that we might unearth versus other places, but when it comes to the written records, we actually have to dig farther and go back to the Ancient Near East and the cuneiform tablets to find records (of) the type of antiquity that we are looking to go to—and those begin about *6000* years ago.

For the purposes of looking back: yeah, it is true that there isn't a lot of literary records prior to the encounters of the Classical world with the Celts to differentiate or determine a traditional academic history concerning the Druids—and all of that which it entails, including these other "Elven" and "Faerie" traditions; all of the Celtic traditions, all of the "Faerie Faiths"... All of that.

And so forth most part, in terms of the "academic world," most historians have left that area alone. It's easier to dig up stuff that's actually older in a place like Egypt and find out things about Egypt than it is to find something out more recently concerning these people in the Celtic lands. And so, again, given that we can't really rely too much on a lot of the Classical records, it's—it really puts us back into being a little bit more intuitive in making comparisons between where we are at and where things were at prior to even the establishment of the European traditions (which we get into in Grade-II; and therein between, we find Route-D, the "Route of Druidism and the Dragon Legacy").

When we consider that the Spirit is eternal, and that these beings, which would have been intermediaries or descendents of, you know, the "Children of Anu," and descendents of "Priest-Kings" and "Dragon-lineages" and so forth, from very distant times. We would assume that they would, of course, have an increased capacity of ability. Knowing this "beingness," they would actually be like, what we would compare as like "high-level Wizard grade" participants [*laughs*] or like "Actualized Technicians," you know, [*laughs*] —what we're calling "A.T." and stuff like that.

The concepts that later get relayed—in terms of the elementals; elemental beings; Elementalism—we know at one point, you know, spiritual entities would have the ability to, you know, choose and discard bodies at will; or even be able to inhabit, for example, you see an increased appreciation for "Nature Mysteries" and the natural traditions as Danubian Druidism goes from being a practice *by* the Elves themselves, the Faerie folk, the Dragon Kings and so forth, and later becomes traditions practiced by a class of Priests or Druids, which is basically dispensing this tradition to the common Celts.

In the beginning, you know, Druidism is *not* the "religion" practiced by, you know, the common Celtic people. Druidism was originally the tradition practiced exclusively by the "highest minds," of which it was later systematized, codified and then we have an establishment of organized society. But at the time, you know—we're looking back, for example, when the "Pheryllt" are present in Wales or the Tuatha d'Anu are showing up in Ireland, okay, we're talking probably 2000 B.C. or so, or prior. And so this is a different point in history—a different point in human populations and the evolution of common culture—than when you just simply take a look back at history from today and see what it had eventually evolved to.

I mean the idea that there's the Otherworld, that there's Faerielands and alternate existences, is pretty common to virtually every ancient tradition; as is the idea that an individual decide to be the Spirit of a "Place"—to locate themselves as, for example, a Guardian Spirit of a particular "locale" or even imbue the point-of-beingness of a "Tree" thereafter. These are not ridiculous concepts—and so we see elements, perhaps of this, intermixed when you read between the lines of what is considered, for example, "Celtic Faerie Lore" or traditions of the "Faerie Faith" and "Elven Druidism" and so forth.

One of the reasons I mention this, is when we deal with Elementals or we talk about the Spirits that are inhabiting Nature and the amount of time that the ancient Druids spent in "communion" and communicating with the natural surroundings, it might begin to make a little bit more sense if we were to apply this additional layer of understanding to it, because clearly these beings were able to "transition" as the, for example, "Milesian Celts" began showing up—and as more and more of the "Human" populations and races and cultures were starting to all push westward and kind of encroach upon these points of the "Faerie Country" and so forth; where they had finally been driven.

For example, that's one of the reasons I was able to trace this migration—like a prehistoric migration—based on the patterns of the La Tene culture, and based on the way which these individuals had set out from the Ancient Near East—whether it was Galatia, like modern-day Turkey or closer to Mesopotamia—but, this evolution would show that as the populations were growing around them, they were moving farther and farther west themselves; and they had reached the western point around the time of, at least, Stonehenge.

And that's why you see a lot of issues with that, concerning what's the classification of "Druids" versus these "Pre-Druidic"—these "Danubians" or the "Pheryllt" of which we considered literally "Druids" by the Greek accounts—so, according to Classical history: the big argument has always been "well, Stonehenge was there at a time before the Druids were there..." And well, I guess that would be true if you consider that the "Druids" were actually only encountered the first time by those other than "Druids" in about 600 B.C. and that's when the Greeks starting writing about them.

You really gotta be careful if you're gonna "history" as "history" and take it from what's someone already familiar with and then start compounding it with a lot of this esoteric history—you really want to be careful, because again: there is only so much that you're gonna be able to point an individual to that's not actually found in some kind of esoteric volume, or you know, "Hidden Secret History of the Such and Such"—there's only so much that contemporary history can really back up.

It's not that there is so much a contradiction between the two, as all the generalizations and conclusions have been based on very fixed parameters of what was already established to be "academic fact." Then of course, changing that at this juncture requires a lot of "inertia"—a lot of energy and momentum—to really make a shift in consciousness, because even changing it one or another book, you know, you can't even really cry out "conspiracy" very much any more; we're able to produce *our* books and materials—they're freely accessible where, you know, books are sold...

So, it's really a matter of placing attentions. Where is an individual placing their attentions during their lifetime as to what's gonna be considered *real* or *acceptable* or within their *reach*. Because most of the time, it's really been diverted everywhere *but* this; and "history" has been treated as such a dry boring subject for so long that most people when they start to realize that any of these esoteric mysteries—if you're going to do it from the ground up—pretty much is an encounter with rigorous history lessons and reconsidering all that's been learned about history; some people become incredibly overwhelmed by that and just sort of this put this aside because it seems like too much to go through.

And so *you* as a "Master" giving them a Master-level understanding, having access to all the materials, having worked through all the materials yourself, should be able to synthesize—watch for the cues and synthesize—a regimen of delivering and communicating the information so that it is consistently within an individual's reach or grasp.

Don't set anything out of reach... When something seems to be indicated as such, it's up to you to quickly shift to... find that point which was missed, where we can go back and kinda get them slowly moving towards that direction. Because some of this stuff does seem incredibly "fanciful" if someone has absolutely no further background; and that's what we're doing here—this is again, this is Grade-I still. So, we're just peeling back the very first layer of what has been laid down upon our understanding of where we've come from and what's led us to where we are today.

And this is just the *First Veil*. We consider it the *Lunar Level*; we consider it the level which has a lot to do with the "magicks" and "enchantments" and the "glamours" of the various lights and elements and symbolism—and all this stuff, which seems like an incredible new world; this is like a whole thing when people finally open to that "all of this is there and exists" and "hey, it can be studied without being a devil worshiper" or some other connotation—it's an entire realm in and of itself; it's its own "continuity" as we've explained; it's its own "level"—its own Grade—entrance into it, it's its own "Gate"; its own "plateau."

So this is really first steps for some people, and to consider it anything it further—that any of this is even taking place in this past and taken place on this planet, just thousands of years ago. It's a place to begin. And so this is why this all falls particularly within the domain of Grade-I.

And then one of the particular benefits of Route-D or Druidism or the "Nature paths" is that it—in terms of the *Pathway to Self-Honesty*—is that it does put one in greater contact or communication with the *Fifth Sphere of Existence*, which is "All Life on Earth" or "All Physical Life," which is one step beyond just treating "Human Life" or the "Human Condition" at the *Fourth Sphere of Existence*. So, it allows someone to begin to operate or *Be* or consider point-of-views or establish lines of communication with that which is actually (quote; unquote) "exterior" to just strictly the "Human" experience.

That's why when you talk about, you know, "shamanism" or some of these "shape-shifting" traditions and lore—what you see is basically the ability to establish a point-of-view; to establish the center of beingness *outside* of a consideration of strictly just the "Human Body" or "Human Condition."

So, you have someone that can basically project—rather than projecting or controlling or commanding the point-of-view and Awareness of just the physical body that they're tied to, the ability to go out an *Be* a "Tree"; to go out and *Be* the "Wolf"; go out and *Be* these other points-of-view, which are points of "beingness" and points of "knowingness." Because again, we know that the highest echelon of "Knowing" is "Being"; and *being* something and *knowing* as a result of *that* point-of-view is essentially [*laughs*] the highest point of Awareness you could have on something.

So that's something that we see—we see in the "Nature traditions"—rather than putting an emphasis on just getting along better in the "physical world" and "what rituals can we do to get a better job in the material existence" and, you know, "how to entice the affections of some..." you know, "...the girl in the neighboring farm" or something like that —it becomes more about an individual path, kind of a "mystic path" where an individual is really reaching out and establishing lines of communication with the material existence around us.

And there is definitely no danger behind this, so long as— like we referred to in previous lectures about other subjects concerning, you know, Grade-I, because it's inherent all through it—that it isn't... it doesn't become simply a matter of finding more of points agreement with the Physical Universe and the fact that the physical and material existence is all there is and that we're entrapped within this particular point-of-view.

The purpose should always be towards "Ascension," and obviously the tools and resources—when you look between the lines, and you have this higher... when you seem to already have the answer key and you look back, it seems to be all laid out there for you; but again, a simple survey of these types of traditions and a simple pass through or just read through with no higher-level comprehension of this stuff, really doesn't get an individual *there*; it doesn't get someone necessarily to these higher points of realization or the ability to understand the concept of being this, and point-of-views and Awareness and all that; relating (it) to Nature, natural surroundings, other lifeforms and so forth—there's no guarantee that a passive or simply a common contemporary survey or participation with these "mysteries" is going to get an individual any further.

There we see, kind of, the boundaries—as I've been trying to explain—of Grade-I or the *First Gate* versus the *Second Gate*. And we're always treating, you know, when we're talking about these "Gates" and "levels" of realization, we're still treating, pretty much the same existence; we're still treating our understanding of universes; we're treating Self; we're treating the concepts of what we can know and what we can do in the directing of energy.

The only difference being exactly what that entails: the parameters and what we're willing to encompass as that understanding; and that just kind of gets bigger and bigger and we move up through these "Spheres" or these "Gates" or these "Levels" or these points of realization and existence; because we're moving *up* and this is the point that we start to see this transition—even in the Mardukite Master Course; because pretty soon here we are encroaching on our Grade-II work.

And Grade-II work for our purposes *does* seem to, pretty much, centralize on the point and geography in history that would be the Ancient Near East—Mesopotamia and Babylon—but the principles, the truths behind all this, as I've tried to explain prior: that which makes any of things effective, and that which has given any of them the ring of truth, carries forth as we move forward—we're able to bring that with us. It isn't a matter of "Oh, well, we spent all this time doing this and that's *all* now nonsense." It really only becomes the case when a person gets stuck on it.

The actual passing through of this knowledge—the moving through of all the Master Course materials—can actually be done quite swiftly and with total comprehension, so long as a person doesn't get too immersed or stuck or hung up on any one the points.

Again, that's another reason for us wanting to deliver the Mardukite Master Course to get instructors empowered and certain in their knowingness—and certain in the materials, and certain in their ability—to be able to relay not only the material to Seekers directly or in an academic or at an Academy level or classroom setting, to also simply to be an assistant to those we, of course, distribute our books to.

Because each of *you* is given the privilege to actually *be* your own distributor of the materials and make this a part of your livelihood and actually increase the Awareness and ability of the Human Condition all around *you* and create it as a sustainable living. And that's one of the reasons for this Mardukite Master Course. Yes, we produce books; yes, I've written and delivered tons of information.

We've reached a point now where we're considered with the delivery of, for example, Mardukite materials—whether it be "Magick," "Druidism," "Systemology," all of that falls under, within, our Mardukite brand. It's not just simply "Marduk" out of Babylon and the Babylonian Tradition. We'll get further into what all that entails—what that means and why this is all incorporated.

But, what I'm intending to deliver and bring together and point out with this Mardukite Master Course, as I tried to explain at the beginning, was not to be just a "verbatim read through" of just "here's what all these texts say, and here's what the next book says, and here's what this book says and there's all the material. Have a nice audiobook." This is meant to relay a wide level of understanding, so that when you are delivering this out there, we are doing this at a professional standard graded level—and that is what we have reached now with the Mardukite Academy of Systemology, which we are now establishing from the underground, but of which we plan to make a more public presence.

In addition to that, we have our religious and spiritual institution as the Church of Mardukite Zuism, which we are currently establishing, again, at this underground level, but we're about to bring that forward to. And so, the purpose of this Mardukite Master Course is to *keep* not only the Mardukite Alumni and those who have been working with us the ten, thirteen, years since the Mardukites were established or followed along as the could, given the work since the 90's, this is about bringing together something that can be professionally delivered.

I want to have, by the end of this course, we want to be able to *"certify"* those that have worked through it that we know have participated in not only hearing thing instructional aspects of the Mardukite Master Course, but also have access to, for example, the outlines and curriculums in your "Instructor's Manual" which is taken from the appendices of these four volumes—the four Master Editions—that we delivered; and to make sure that those that are representing us, and those that have these materials, and those that are willing to participate in this... "Mass Ascension Project" [*laughs*] I guess, that we're undertaking for the 2020's and potentially beyond, that we're all on the same page, that we have a good understanding of it, that it's a mutual understanding as far as what the intention was behind it.

You're of course [*laughs*] entitled to your own opinions and to discover what works for you and what works for your Seeker—but the important part is that we have this standard to deliver and that your personal experiences and your personal inclinations—your personal opinions and, we know, we try to eliminate as much of the "reactive programming" in our Pilots and Instructors before we just turn them loose on the world, but given that that's not one-hundred percent the case—it's important that we've demonstrated that the Mardukite Master Course is a fixed set of material that an individual can access, whatever edition it is, it's going to still fall within the standards and curriculum outline of this material.

This way nobody is getting lost on it and it's really up to you, watching the cues of your Seekers that you're working with—to determine the direction and flow of this information; for *you* to have a complete understanding of it; for your to be able to *relay* it as best applied; and to be sure that your personal inclinations and experiences aren't ever getting in the way of that: the clear transmission and duplication of this material, because this is important for *these* Grades of material.

And then of course, we start to deal with a similar aspect of that once we get into the "Flight Schools" of Systemology Piloting and other "Advanced Processes" and "Wizard Grade" stuff that we're gonna be able to do—and I plan to release a completely separate course on that—but for this, we are talking about "Master-level" instruction and we are talking about the ability to *be* a "Master-level Instructor." And this doesn't necessarily include Advanced Systemology or Piloted Procedures.

: LECTURE 20—OTHERWORLD TECH :
(September 23, 2020)

The "Route of Druidism and the Dragon Legacy" is actually of such richness and color that you really could formulate a "Druid School" exclusively from that—or at least, quite an extensive curriculum for your "Wizard School." In fact, it's been designed in such a way, that for example, *Merlyn's Complete Book of Druidism* and the Master materials that compose this, is actually a qualifying "Grade-I" access-point for those that seek it—for those that prefer this to the broader study of the "magical curriculum" and "ritual magick" and "ceremonial traditions" of all that in the Western Magical Tradition (that are explored in Route-A).

Honestly, this has been designed, and this textbook here—this Master Edition—has been designed, so that if necessary, *this* can be someone's both introduction to "Magick & Mysticism" in addition to the "Route of Druidism & Dragon Legacy" that leads into Grade-II. So, there really is no enforcement...

Now, *you* being a "Master Instructor" and this being the "Master Course" and to be *"Certified"* in being able to instruct all Grades is to *know* all Grades, but when it comes to individual Seekers and it comes to bringing those onto the *Pathway to Self-Honesty* or as those enter into Mardukite Zuism or even the Academy of Systemology or the Systemology Society, we don't actually require that an individual work through Route-A. It does make exceptional reference material and background and a core foundation for doing the rest—there is no substitute, single source substitute for *The Great Magickal Arcanum* out there today.

But for those who end up—their introduction or their entry-point onto the *Pathway*—ends up being the "Nature Magic,"

"Druidism," the "Dragon Tradition," "Celtic Faerie," any of this... just go ahead and use this as the Grade-I work and emphasize that which they're showing the inclinations in.

The reason I point this out, also, is because I promised you we'd end today with a lecture on some kind of "Magic Tech" or "Ritual Tech" or "Druid Tech," so I just wanted to point that out: that there *is* [are] elements to incorporate a "magical curriculum" specifically from this Druidic Tradition, or this presentation of it.

I prepared—and this was one of the, if you want to know, one of the original versions of the "Book of Shadows" or "Book of Lights & Enchantments" as we called it in the "Elven Fellowship Circle of Magick"—the "*Elven-Druid Grimoire*" is the middle section, or one of the Books, within the *Elvenomicon* or *Merlyn's Complete Book of Druidism*.

And the "*Elven-Druid Grimoire*" is essentially a complete "ritual guide" for an individual to follow their traditional use of "practical magick," "ritual magic"—the same kind of flavor of work that we were discussing previously (a couple days ago). It's essentially an entire "Book of Shadows" or "*grimoire*" for doing this within the "Elven-Faerie" or "Faerie-Druid" tradition.

And so what you will find in here—in addition to the layout of the "Elements" and the kind of "Elemental" *schema* of how they're arranged and set up—you'll find information on the "Casting of a Circle of Power," the "Calling of the Elementals" at each of the directions, the "Operations of the Magic Circle," "Closing the Magic Circle" at the end, "Consecrating Ritual Tools," "Consecrating Representations of the Gifts of Faerie" that I was describing (in a previous lecture today); also using ritual magic to assist one, like, operating in Nature, to basically increase one's channels of communication—the flow—between the individual, the Elf or the Druid or the Faerie or however you want to refer to the *practitioner*, and Nature.

Most of the "Druid Magic" and "Elven Magic"—at least within this tradition—is concerned with that. And so you see a lot of emphasis on incorporating Nature or communing with Nature, spending time in Nature, observing Nature, in order to essentially be "grounded." Grounding being one of the core fundamentals of operating any other work. And any other work can be done from, you know, as an Actualized Alpha-Spirit.

All you need to be doing is making sure you're grounded and in complete communication, control and command of the body; and then be able to operate from the point-of-view of the Alpha-Spirit. And this could easily be done when working in Nature, free of a lot of the worldly distractions, free of any disturbances—being able to achieve the first core of any higher-level work, which is essentially *grounding* and *centeredness* and being able to move out from there.

We see that emphasis within any of the ritual texts or the "magick" that's presented in here. And then also "Self-dedication Ceremonies," "Personal Initiations," "Initiations Into An Elven Group"—that's all found in here. And "Group Ceremonial Applications," which can be used to observe, if you wish to observe some kind of "ceremonial" marking of the various times of year and the various traditional "festivals" and Celtic holidays and stuff, there's plenty of material for that within here.

It's really all self-explanatory; no reason for me to go through those specific points at all. It's really based on the inclination of what dramaticized practice that one wishes to add; and then of course, never losing sight of that pursuit of the *magic behind the magic* as we move up the *Pathway of Self-Honesty.*

Now in terms of any "Magic Tech," "Ritual Tech"—anything along those lines; practical applications—when it comes to Druidry: Druidism—and this is why I introduce it *secondary* to, for example, Route-A—is that Druidism is a little bit more "intuitive" in its applications of the "mystical traditions." In fact, it's a little bit more of a "mystical" tradition than a "magical" tradition.

We start to see the, like a bridge on that element—but it's really routed in the authority of the individual as Self and their empowerment, their understanding, their realization, and their ability to be in a state of *knowing* true knowledge, that enables and empowers their skills and abilities and what they do went they go about treating the natural world, okay? Which is a little bit different from the more rigorous ritual ceremonial formulas and particular times of day and astrological signs, in which we see other traditions a little bit more fixed in what they are intending to do in their ritual texts or their "magick."

So, in this case, you're dealing with, really, not as much of a rigorous roll-call of "rules" and "requirements" and "steps" as you are establishing, again, that personal relationship—that personal communion—with Nature, with the natural Elements, with, you know, basically the "Cosmos" in essence, as you move your way up. In that relationship—in that knowingness—being able to have a better mastery and control of the experience of the material world.

In terms of the "New Age" concept of accessing, you know, the "Faerieland" or so forth, what you'd find in most "New Age How-To" books—most of which involve some sort of mental or astral travel, (but) it's really descriptive scripts: what they refer to as "guided meditations." I mean, you'll find just books *filled*, hundreds of pages, of guided meditations—almost just reads like a "novel" of stuff. I mean, I don't know what... if they intended to record them and have them played back or you're supposed to remember all this stuff or just read through them, because honestly, probably the biggest benefit you'd have in reading through them—or any use whatsoever—is that they might be actually "restimulative" to some kind of memory or past-life thing or some experience that's been forgotten or filtered out.

But, you know, you could just as soon get that same stuff reading anything else or just watching many of the shows or movies that are available out there—would almost yield the same effect, and that's basically just increasing the acceptance or Awareness or concept or possibility or parameter within the realm of mental imagery, or within the realm of reality—within the realm, grasp, hold and reach of what's considered possible, that someone may be able to have these, kinda, "Gates" or "access points" open up to them.

Because prior to that, until someone knows it's, again, possible or real or any actual aspect to it, then there is nothing to behold. Suddenly an individual begins to read novels or watch TV or play various fantasy-oriented games, all of which have these certain themes or whatnot, it very well may end up "restimulating" certain imprints, certain programming, various implants—even past-life recall—concerning not only times here on this planet when such things were present or there was more mysticism or certain themes or icons were present, but also in other civilizations and times on this planet and even distant pasts and even *before* incarnations on *this* Earth and so on and so forth.

It's for those reasons that some people get... you've heard of some of the "dangers" or you've seen the propaganda about some of the "inherent dangers" to some of this; and that's really all it is. Those who aren't really able to *handle* some of the mental imagery or the triggers of the "restimulation" of who they are—sometimes really have, without guidance, and again this is where a Master would really come in handy, they begin to lose themselves in it; or they lose touch with what's really going on, because they "restimulate" something, which is very real to them, and it was probably very real when it happened, but it's not present right now, is it?

And so a lot of times individuals get kind of "keyed in" or "trapped" or "locked into" specific modes because they've been "turned on" and they're being handled as if it's happening *now*, because for whatever reason it wasn't handled at the time or it hasn't been managed or it's been suppressed to the point where it's—the pressures are just, it can't be ignored anymore.

But one way or another, it has to be faced and handled, and so what you're actually doing when—I mean, as we step back through these various traditions and histories and then even going into Mesopotamia and where some of the implanting for *this* current civilization first occurred—you are definitely running into many elements that could be "restimulative," that could trigger various responses, reactions or even complete "phase-shifts" to where someone as been, you know, flipped on like a switch, that they're trying to handle this other stuff that obviously have suddenly come up.

Now *you* from a Grade-III perspective—as a Systemologist—is actually able to treat these circumstances and this phenomenon, you know, far better and more effective and valuable to a Seeker, than we have ever been able to do before when we were only working with these systems and traditions within, what we would consider, the Grades they are in now.

Being true to this idea that we're treating a Master Course level or Master-level understanding of anything that could be considered "practical tech" or "authentic tech" in this level (or in this area), really it would be impossible to sidestep at least one case study that *is* explored within *Book of Elven-Faerie* material; and that's, of course, the Life of Robert Kirk.

Robert Kirk, or Reverend Robert Kirk—this is a 17th Century "case study" that we use to explore one of the ways in which the encounters between "mortals" and "Elves." And Robert Kirk—he was born in 1644—he was the seventh son of an Episcopalian minister; he was born in Scotland. Now, he also became a minister; he was known as Reverend Robeert Kirk—and his main interest during his lifetime, was not only, as far as missionary work, not only the preservation of the Gaelic-Welsh language, but also, in doing so, participating in the Gaelic translation of the "*Holy Bible.*"

We've seen other examples of this by the Bardic Culdee—for example, the *Book of Kells*, which is an "illuminated manuscript." It's basically the "Four Gospels" in the Gaelic language with all the illuminated and colorful calligraphy and spiral artwork and so forth of the Celtic tradition.

Really, what he's known for—much more than any translation work on the *Bible*—is a book called "*The Secret Commonwealth of Elves, Fauns & Faeries.*" And this is actually one of the few real reference points that an individual has when exploring any kind of historical background for revival of, for example, the "Elven Tradition"—the "Faerie Tradition"—because in that material we learn about such things as the Seelie Court and Unseelie Court, the Faerie Courts, Faerie Traditions, beliefs, practices, customs—things regarding the "Faerie."

Much of (this) is actually synthesized in the material for the *Elvenomicon*. It's not a baseless tradition that I was establishing—much like we're doing in Mardukite Zuism in bringing Mesopotamian tradition and aspects and explorations of our most ancient literature that we have on the planet into the "Neopagan" realm. What I was doing with the *Book of Elven-Faerie* and the *Elvenomicon* material was essentially integrating a complete tradition concerning Elven and Faerie Druidism and these practices.

And so much of the work is actually synthesized from remnants of actual lore. And rather than the Druidry that's presented as philosophical in some of the other portions—for example, the *Druid's Handbook*—in the *Elvenomicon*, the lore and the tradition and the way that the ritual texts are written out, are all derived from the researched explorations of mine concerning the "Faerie Faith" and various

"Celtic Elvish" traditions and this legacy.

With Robert Kirk's work—now, you gotta remember: his work is being presented as... don't forget, he's a member of the clergy—and he's writing particularly for a nation that is predominantly Christianized; and so most of the explorations and any of his personal encounters or opinions are actually passed off as being those of, for a example, a "seer" or "according to an account of interview" with someone.

But, his legacy and his interaction with the Faerie Folk—if we are to assume that his journals and that which is otherwise not published is considered valid—is that he had a direct relationship and encounter with this Faerieland Otherworld; and that this was not once, but on repeated occasions. He was allowed there with a sketch-diary-journal and make accounts of his explorations, or at the very least, was able to leave with enough memory or knowledge of it that he was able to quickly put it down.

He was permitted to really have an access to information that—you know, *we* can derive a lot of Faerie lore and what is considered "common knowledge" about various traditions and beliefs and mythology *now*, but his exploration of this and his delivery of this and accounts far exceed anything that was really available to him at that time. And now a lot of it, as I said, has become commonplace.

Best we can tell from 1688 until 1692, he basically was having some kind of four-year long actual initiatory encounter —or initiation—into the Otherworld, this Faerieland and was able to actually make a record of much that he was able to discover as a result of that. And he really... The thing that is interesting about this is it's not something that he really presented during his lifetime; it was not something that was divulged; it's nothing that he capitalized on.

Even the *Secret Commonwealth* that he was known for; it wasn't even published during his lifetime. And so, you know, really this.. whatever was done or whatever his experience was, was specific to himself. Anything that we draw from it, we draw from it *after the fact*, basically going back into this guy's life, but as far as his own accounts and the information that he was able to draw forth from it, he certainly was not trying to delude anybody or anything of that nature.

And he never actually in what he was preparing perhaps at one point to publish—because it was never necessarily completed or published afterward in a complete state—he wasn't intending to make any claims to anything personally. So, any of his encounters and so forth were entirely his own, which he later based writings on which he would deliver some point, I guess, "exoterically." [*Laughs*]

We do know that other than the idea of trees—because trees are always considered a gateway or an access point, when it comes to Nature mysteries—what Reverend Kirk was actually working with, what he would actually approach and then give a certain knock and then access, was what we know today to be called a "Faerie Mound" or "burial mound," an ancient ancestral "burial mound" in Scotland. And these were known as "Faerie Hills" and they had a long tradition—a long legacy—for example, the locals would tell children, you know, "Don't get caught going to close to the Fairy Hills," you know, things of that nature.

These places had already an inherent... people knew there was something about them; that there was something different about them or that they had a certain significance. These beliefs have shifted and changed throughout time. Various cultures and various religious paradigms come in and have various beliefs about it.

But at the time, and still today in many rural areas of the Celtic countries, you still see this and although today we consider a lot of this "superstition" and so forth—even historically; even sometimes in the metaphysical realm—because honestly, just because people have inclinations or interests in the New Age or the metaphysical and so forth, it doesn't mean they're necessarily "open" to all of the parameters and phenomenon that are inherent within it.

Because some of it lies outside of the semantic-set they're most concerned with; for example, any kind of connection to the "Faerie Folk" or the races or legacies that these were derived from—and for example, "astral" or "Otherworldly" or "inter-dimensional" and other aspects that we find even more, for example, in Mesopotamia and Grade-II and the Celestial Pantheons, which these figures all throughout the world—whether they were "Elementals" or certain "Dragon Kings" or priest lineages—they were all said to be descendents *of*, derived *of*, derived *from.*

And there being part of the "Authority" and "Power" again—because the "magick" and mysticism, as we move upward through these Grades here, moving from Route-A into Route-D and then Grade-II—these are... the concept of "practical mysticism" or "metaphysics" or "magick" or "spirituality" or "religion" or however it is treated is... well, right there: it's treated differently in each respect.

In this instance: this is based again on certain matter of authority and relationship encounter concerning Robert Kirk and his access to the Otherworld and the Seelie and his eventual encounter with the Unseelie Court.

What ends up eventually happening which is, in some ways kinda disturbing, is that he ended up trespassing, I guess, in the Unseelie territory while out there. And as a result of his encounter with this Dark Elf, he's actually sentenced to "death" so to speak—and instead is actually claimed... he's vouched for, and so they eventually decide that he can be a prisoner, and then forever inhabit what was referred to as the "Lands Below."

And so in *his* accounts and the interactive threshold or portal between the worlds being these mounds, the Faerieland is referred to as the "Lands Below," and the surface world—that which is, like, the physical world of humanity and where things take place on the surface of the Earth is called the "Lands Above." And so that's the distinction of the, you know, the term "Otherworld" isn't used; that's one of *my* catch-words that I sometimes apply—and then "Faerieland" is simply, again, another of the terms that we use when we are describing this.

But, it was the "Lands Above" and the "Lands Below"—so, he was basically sentenced to serve out his existence in the "Lands Below." So, he's given the time to set his affairs in order; he's given one night to return to the "Lands Above" on good faith, of course, that he's going to come back to serve his sentence. And so he prepared the manuscripts and journals and sketchbooks and what he had, basically, for his son—to be passed down to his son.

What we know to be the case is that that night his body was later found next to the "Faerie Hill." And so therein, we can't even be absolutely certain of the nature of the transitioning—it's very possible that his encounters with the Otherworld (or the Lands Below or this Faerie Realm), not to say it's not real, but to say that it was not necessarily "terrestrial"; that is was not necessarily that a (physical) "doorway" opened up and he literally walked down beneath the "soil."

Because one of the things he does note is that the "Lands Below" were actually very similar—if not more vivid—to the Lands Above; that it had its own sky, that it had its own skyscapes that changed with night and day and so forth. And so from that we would have to assume that it's perhaps a different dimension; and for all intents and purposes *probably* the "Magical Universe," that we only really touch on in the Master Course, but of which we're exploring much more deeply at higher Systemological levels.

And so in terms of "*beings,*" we know that this Other existence—we know that it is possible to transition between existences and that *beings* have an ability to inhabit or take on physical bodies or genetic vehicles as needed.

But, we don't know for certain that in most instances—without being fully Actualized; without being to a point where an individual could pick up and set down the command of bodies and continue on an existence and later pick it up again and so on and so forth.

We don't know that these were literally physical transitions into an Otherworld as a "body" or that each time that Reverend Kirk was encountering—and later inhabiting this Faerieland during these encounters—that his "body" wasn't being left back here and that this wasn't just simply a very surrealistic use of "transference of the point-of-view."

Because again, this would be the ability to actually "exteriorize" from the "interior" of the Human Condition; and the condition that you would have to be maintaining only the point-of-view of Awareness of a physical body—and then being able to transition that point; being able to actually occupy this other higher existence, which if we consider the "Descent of Universes"—we consider any kabbalistic model or any layered cosmology, the chakras and all this stuff—we would assume that basically there is this part between the original state of the Alpha-Spirit (wherever it resides as basically a peak point or island on a complete Infinity), that its essence has moved through these successive universes and that there is a certain trail or track or a certain timeline taking effect as certain imprints and incidents are given emotional mass and consideration and imprinting and implanting each step of the way.

So, it's very possible then, that each and every one of us that's occupying a consideration of a point-of-view of the Human Condition in *this* existence, has formerly occupied in this other existence.

And for most people, the memory of this has been blotted out—and of course any ability or responsibility and control over it, and the ability to move between universes or even to occupy this other higher universe that we once occupied before descending to the considerations that we should be in this lower one, and forgetting that we were making that choice; that these are conscious decisions or consequences of considerations along the way.

And one of the keys—one of the higher level keys behind any of this work, when we consider what's possible or what's taken place—is that we are trying to move back to that point from this point. And to do so would be very much mirroring what we consider the *Pathway to Self-Honesty* or the *Ladder of Ascension*. And so in that, we can see a mirror of us getting back to these roots—getting back to what... calling the *is* what *is* and actually getting to the heart of where we came from, where this legacy has been left behind and set down, so that we might follow that map and a route back out.

[*Okay, we'll call that good for this evening. And we see everyone back here, bright and shinning, early tomorrow. We're gonna be working towards unlocking the Second Gate and transitioning from Grade-I to Grade-II.*]

: LECTURE 21—NATURAL PATHS :
(September 24, 2020)

[Okay, this is the twenty-first lecture of the Mardukite Master Course; September 24, 2020. We got a new "program schedule" for you—I have extended the Course lecture structure from 40-lectures to 48-lectures; so, by the lunch period, we should be halfway through; transitioning from Grade-I into Grade-II; or the material from Gate-One to the realm of Gate-Two by lunch period.]

There are, of course, now two particular facets remaining of Grade-I material—particularly of Route-D, the "Route of Druidism and the Dragon Legacy" that we've still not really touched on in the Mardukite Master Course. One of them, of course, being trees, the Ogham and the woodland forest "magick system" and the magical lore of the Elves and Faerie lore; and also again, as mentioned in the definition or title of the Route, the "Dragon Legacy."

And it's the "Dragon Legacy" that under-runs—it's a current that essentially under-runs everything we have discussed concerning the Elven Tradition, the Faerie Traditions, Otherworld Tech, anything from the *Elvenomicon*, anything actually from the Druid work, and was really an underlying basis even in the Western Magical Tradition. So, it's the "Dragon Legacy"—that element of Grade-I—that particularly bridges directly to Grade-II and the origins of the Dragon Legacy in the Ancient Near East and, of course, our emphasis on Mesopotamia.

Both the "Tree Work" and "Dragon Work" (the "Dragon Legacy"; "Dragon Tradition") and anything else involving trees, forests, Nature... That doesn't just mean the most dense forest woodlands that you might be conjuring to mind.

When we refer to elemental and Elven and Faerie traditions, we're also talking about any terrains that have their own connotation in terms of "Elemental Realms."

Of course, with Nature and Earth, when we're dealing with herbs and plants and stones and trees—of course, it begs the question right there: because we're talking about Earth; the Earth Element. Of course, the Earth (planet) being composed of an entire "elemental system" however, so we include some of these other aspects as well. And we cover that in the "Elemental" discussions and there's plenty of Elemental lore regarding that within the textbooks.

What we find is also an affinity to other terrains as well. We also have the mountains—the mountain areas—which are connected to Fire as are the deserts. And there's the prairies, there's swamps—any kind of geographical natural terrain that you could consider, has its own qualities, its own elemental composure and then, of course, its own associations when we talk about correspondences or allocating various energetic attributes to it.

Most of the "Nature Magic," woodland magic, Ogham lore, all of that, I reserved for the materials of *Elvenomicon*—what used to be the *Book of Elven-Faerie*—because I wanted to focus the *Druid's Handbook* exclusively on the broad elements of the philosophy and tradition, just as we covered a couple days ago, or yesterday rather—the early morning lectures.

And then, of course, the Dragon Legacy: we have this material called the *Draconomicon*, and we'll get into that later when we start to emphasize the "Dragon Legacy" specifically—and that's actually introduced in *Elvenomicon*: the concept that the Dragon Legacy and its links back to Mesopotamia, that is actually introduced in the *Elvenomicon*. And all of these materials are, of course again, available in our Grade-I Route-D Master Edition textbook, which is *Merlyn's Complete Book of Druidism: A Master Course in Druidry for Modern Druids*.

One of the key elements of this type of work—if we're looking at the broader picture of the *Pathway to Self-Honesty*, and I mentioned this only briefly before—is that all this work is dealing with encounters with what we consider in Systemology the "Fifth Sphere of Existence" or the "Fifth Sphere of Beingness," where we are moving beyond simply point-of-views or aspects specific or restricted to a paradigm or a Mind-System specific to, again, the Human Condition. We basically cut the Human Condition off at "Four" when it comes to that model; and we'll run that through here just briefly—it kind of runs parallel with our Standard Model, but it's not completely one-to-one. It's just two ways in which we've used a "seven-plus-one" paradigm to establish this "model" of wholeness.

And so we start with Self, the individual. The individual is then dealing with aspects beyond Self where they're dealing with domestic survival; the ability to extend beyond Self and begin to establish—so we're dealing with family, we're dealing with domestic situations and so forth. Beyond that, we have the Third Sphere, which is composed of various families or various individuals setting up their own homes—and that would be any kind of group; whether it be societies, the communities, the neighborhoods; or even a group such as the Mardukite Academy—anywhere where it is composed of these various aspects where an individual has set up their own home, their own domestic epicenter.

And then of course, if we consider all the groups in society that are possible, we get to the Fourth—which is essentially the Human Condition; which is everything that could be composed or contained within the Human Condition. And the reason why some people have associated this kind of incorrectly—to try and compare it to our Standard Model—is that the Standard Model, the "MCC" or Master Control Center (which is the Mind-System Control Center) is basically restricted to the Human Condition; it's operated by a Spirit, but the Mind itself is very much specific to the Human Condition.

And then we talk about—in higher levels of Systemology—actually going outside of the Mind, or going "outside of" or "exterior" to the Human Condition, rather than the "interior mechanisms" of the Mind-System as it applies to beta-existence.

So that's why we have the "One-Two-Three-Four" there for that "model," and it just so happens to coincide that the Fourth Sphere—when we use this system of logic or "Venn diagrams" [*laughs*] or however you want to refer to these concentric circular models—we then reach, again, a point where Humans on Earth are *one* element or *one* group or *one* facet of simply All Life on Earth, which would be the Fifth Sphere; and that, again, would be composed of what you'd consider the Green World of Nature; you're talking about the animals; you're talking about plants and trees; you're talking about all organic life—and even the Earth as a living organism or a system, which would then be a part of *other* systems when we bring it up farther along.

What this is.. What this work is doing is putting someone in touch with something outside of the strict confines of the Human Condition. So, I mean, even at a practical level—if you're talking about trying to get *outside* of, or sidestep, or kind of release one's Self of the trapping and worries and concerns of the mundane material world—it's easy to step outside of that... take your first steps anyways—reach that on a "mental level" even—by going into Nature; by identifying with energies and concepts and mental imagery that is not restricted to simply the "humanistic civilized world."

And so that's where you see a difference between the "Natural Philosophies" and (the) different "mysticism" that were meant to start elevating the individual out of the confines of the Human systems, as opposed to some of these other—which we've already covered kind of briefly in previous lectures—various traditions of "magick" and systems of "ritualism" that were really more geared towards trying to get along better in the material aspects of the universe.

Rather than liberating an individual, for example, from compulsive desires or underlying thought fragmentation, these other traditions have a tendency of just amplifying those and making those stronger—rather than *dealing* with reactive-response mechanisms, an individual ends up "supercharging" the programming that they're already kinda running.

And so if you can access these higher points of Awareness and *Beingness* from within the Grade-I system—which is really [*laughs*] more easy to access through Route-D directly than Route-A—you'll then have basically reached pinnacle of what we're trying to establish with Grade-I, because it's not necessarily—it's not a Grade that we're trying to impose "Oh, memorize all these grimoires and here's every different ritual tradition out there and try them all and practice them all..."

It's really getting (them) to a point of establishing *what* they are—and we keep using that phrase, you know, "*is*-ing what it *is*" and being basically able to call this stuff out; be able to know it (and) not have a lot of "mystery" enshrouded with it.

Once we can, kind of, *flatten* or *crunch* this concept of "Mystery" concerning the material world, the physical structure of the world, the systems of civilization and so forth, it's easier to step passed that and start looking beyond.

An individual can either focus on "themselves" as a point of *Beingness* and simply emphasize strict regimens, such as we might do in Grade-III, of Self-Development and Self-Actualization with exercises and "processing" that's focused directly at themselves—or at this point, we're reaching out to this "Fifth Sphere" as a way of basically moving passed the *Second*, the *Third*, the *Fourth*—and *seeing* how they all work together as a mechanistic system.

We don't displace Self in the process of that, but again: it's two different routes of working at the Systemology of existence. And in this instance, when we're dealing with the "Route of Druidism," we're looking at Nature.

[So, for the remaining few lectures, we'll focus specifically on the "Natural Paths" and some of the lore that is connected to that and some of the practical tech that can be drawn from that—and then, again, we'll move into the Dragon Legacy, the material of the *Draconomicon* and find ourselves in Mesopotamia by the end of the day.]

Obviously the Druids spent a lot of time in Nature—and any kind of "Elven" or "Faerie" work or any kind of tradition that we might attach to that is related to the same. And so many of the aspects of their tradition, of course, are tied specifically to concepts of Nature.

One of the most commonly derived—you'll find "divination" sets of this; you'll find correspondences of this in virtually all of the "Celtic Magic" and "Druidic" books out there in the mainstream—but the Ogham (Ogam); the Ogham Alphabet is something we find specifically linked to the Druids of the Celts. Although it's sometimes referred to as the "Celtic Tree Alphabet": each of these characters represented not only a "tree" but many other—just as the tarot represented many other correspondences and aspects of esoterica as essentially, like, a pathway; which is something of higher-level understanding of the "Tarot," and the paths of even the way it was interpreted (with) the "kabbalah"—these all link back to the ancient Star-Gates and the ancient mysteries from the original Mystery School and bringing these to new levels.

Unfortunately, we found that many—many have found the paradigms to be very restrictive—so, unfortunately, the Ogham, if an individual is only looking at it for the "divinatory" aspects as, like, a runic system of trees, it never really gets treated much farther than that. The same as with the

Tarot, or even with the Kabbalah, which is obviously incorporated into *so many* of the modern—the structure of grimoires and the pantheons of spirits and the way in which the Western Magical Tradition was eventually interpreted—that a lot of this gets lost.

To present this as another system—we want to make sure we are looking at it specifically from the Druidic paradigm; and that it does have applications to other elements, but that for this particular Grade, we're going to look at it in connection to Druidry and its Nature mysteries.

Now, as we move farther up into—even outside of Grade-III—and we've discovered the implanting of the Human Condition, the manner in which the "goals" and "desires" and "compulsions" and different "phases" of "identity" have been taken on between this lifetime—other lifetimes—we understand that these are actually all reflective of a higher understanding; that these *Pathways*—whether they're "21 Keys of the Tarot" or the "21 Ogham Fedh ("fews"), they are referred to as Fedh ("Fews") in the original language here—that these are actually representing different stages, different archetypes, different personality programs and different identities which have been assumed, and that these are all in connection to each other: that we've run down this incredible chain of existences going through however many countless universes, through the Magic Universe, into this physical beta-existence that is mainly occupied by "Dark Space."

And so these actually represent these "ladders" and "pathways"—are actually meant to represent something much much higher, of which it's very seldom that this is tapped into. Even the "planes" or "Enochian aethyrs" that are encountered in *that* system—the way that it's been presented, strictly in the Grade-I presentation—and this includes all mainstream materials on the market today, those that you would find typically being advertised more heavily or just appearing in virtually ever single local bookstore—these are really meant to focus on the lowest levels of knowledge that are accessible from these "mysteries."

I don't want to extend Grade-I, in terms of these lectures, farther than it needs to be to relay the materials, because we have other higher level stuff to get to, but it's important for me to stop at each of these points, because rather than having someone just read through these books, that we've again, in the course of twenty-five years and now tapping into the higher Wizard Grades of Systemology now, and the expansion of Mardukite Zuism and the way we've been able to interpret ancient mysteries and the ancient tablets, there's no reason for me to continue to propagate that this (Grade-I) material is all that there is in understanding.

It's all that we can determine for certain, when we consider the relay verbatim of these traditions as they are passed down through hundreds and thousands of years into common "New Age" literature—but I don't want to make any mistakes, or have any Seekers here, or Instructors, make any mistakes in thinking that we have not evolved our knowledge any further than what these texts have presented.

Keep in mind, again, when it comes to the Mardukite Master Course, when it comes to the relay of this "graded path" that we've set up, and the *Pathway to Self-Honesty*, and the way the Grades are now situated in terms of the Master Course, the way that the materials are laid out in terms of the various routes an individual can take—these are just simply entry-points.

And we're not trying to overwhelm someone with the First Grade of material, when we're dealing with the *Lunar Level* of just rising above the Earth Gate and seeing there is a world of "enchantments" and "mysticism" out there that is overlaying it, which has otherwise been screened or filtered or blocked from the traditional everyday Awareness of, you know, commonplace society: the standard-issue surface world society that is taking place around us.

Whether you're dealing with "Norse Runes" or you're dealing with the "Celtic Ogham" or you're dealing with any representation of these ancient mysteries—they've all been referred to—even the "Tarot" (as Crowley was trying to get across in his *Book of Thoth*). This is a book of knowledge, of keys, of wisdom, that has been basically left behind as a series of symbols as a substitution for whatever it is that was being represented.

Each of these pathways—each of these levels—is meant to be essentially faced and *flattened*, just like what we've been doing along the way in the materials of the Mardukite Master Course; and what we continue to do up the way as we deal with not only the last 6000 years of development of *modern* Human civilization, but the actual essence of the individual —the Alpha-Spirit, the I-AM—the individual that is occupying Awareness and a point-of-view of the Human Condition.

But the I-AM is not the Human Condition *nor* is it the "Mind." The Spirit—the Self—is no more the "Mind" than it is the "Body." These are just other "systems" that are being used an interrelated. And so when we look at the structure of them—the structure of systems—this has basically been tackled by "systematizers" for thousands of years; whether it be the ancient Babylonian system of "Ladder of Lights"— the Gateways—or it's derivations of the same knowledge into other Kabbalahs and other fragments of it into various steps and paths and keys.

These are all representative of the same ideal. And the only way in which any of it is effective is if it's actually delivering an individual up the *Pathway*, you know, into Ascension to higher levels of realization and through the higher Gates of understanding. Otherwise, most of this knowledge—when treated, even by other Magic Schools; others that, you know, that we may even be considered in competition with in the underground and so forth—others... it really remains fixed at the Grade-I level. Even if it pierces or makes hints to or eventually sometimes accidentally falls to [*laughs*] realizations that can actually access into the *Second Gate*—into the Second Plane.

Really most of the material that has been presented... even using the Ogham specifically as an example as an alternative to a "runic" system or Tarot divination, is really only gonna get [*laughs*] an individual so far. These in and of themselves *are* "tools" that can be used for Self-realization, but they really are meant to open one up to new levels of realization that far surpass what is relayed verbatim in Grade-I material. And therein you find what is often considered, for example, the "Secrets of the Druids" or the "Secrets of the Arcanum" or "Hidden Knowledge."

Because no matter how it's relayed in print—within these paradigms; within looking at it... within these structured systems at a Grade-I level—the true "mysteries" or the true "secret" (because it is no "mystery")—the true realizations —that illuminate all this are not found within the "printed word"; they're not found within the "symbols" themselves; they're not found within anything that can *be* sold or delivered just widely in that respect.

It's an individual effort; an individual interest; an individual application of attention that's going to actually deliver someone—a Seeker—to higher levels of realization; not specifically "book learning."

Now as opposed to small clay tokens that you might find in Mesopotamia or in other areas that—for example small "Norse Runes" that might have been carved on small stones —one of the ways in which the Ogham script has been used *in* the Druidic tradition by the Bardic (tradition) in both the Welsh and Irish forms of Druid lore that we still have present today—is that they were carved or burned, are the two ways in which it would be done; but it was done on wood.

And this was either done on wood—you could either use like, you know, a "wood chip" to make, if you're more familiar with the "runestone" style of divination, or what was more common is that they would be carved on small sticks. And usually these were sticks that were essentially the same size and filed down and stripped and dressed.

The Ogham Sticks can be used, also, for divination—and the other thing being that there's this concept of "cryptomancy" that comes up in ancient "Hermetic" lore, about discerning "secret names" or words: that to know something's name was to be able to have a command over it. You see prior to incanting a lot of "Divine Names" and a lot of the rigorous magick and grimore magick—you see in these older traditions, the actual *diving* of them; where they didn't have a roll-call of spirits or, you know, the kind of catalogs that you see in the grimoires today; that all of Nature and the forces and the command of the cosmos and so on and so forth, was dependent on an individual's relationship and their own understanding—their ability to be in contact with, to communicate with, and have a reality on, these various aspects...

Rather than when you start to see the "magic" evolve through the Middle Ages and into the secret recesses where the underground cabals and the "Mystery Schools" are established during the times of persecution—the persecution of Christianity. You see an emphasis more on the rigorous study—volumes and volumes and volumes of books that have to be gone through—because there was no way to preserve this "secret knowledge" and just put it out there in such a way that it could be perverted or stolen by the Church or other aspects of that.

In the beginning, prior to all this rigorous academic intellectualization of occult and "magick" and the esoteric and metaphysical studies, the more ancient paths—the more shamanic and indigenous and Nature-oriented paths—would simply do it by observation. So, this is where you find natural philosophy and the origins of what later became the physical sciences, but originally practiced as natural philosophy; and practiced through observation, direct knowing—we've been saying all throughout this: that the highest echelon of knowing is being.

And so we see a lot of transference in the mysticism and magick of Druidry: the transference of point-of-view into various trees and animals and different forms. This is even, kind of—if you look at the "*Sword in the Stone*," the kind of more "Disney" version of the Arthurian Druidic apprenticeship of King Arthur by Merlyn—one of the key elements of T.H. White's novels that was used for that is Arthur being transformed into, for example, a fish or a squirrel, or in the case of the novels, for example in the "*Book of Merlyn*" (which is the unpublished conclusion to the "*Once and Future King*." It's since been published—but it wasn't part of the "*Once and Future King*" series of books that the "*Sword in the Stone*" is excerpted from originally), Arthur is transformed into an ant—and basically sent into the "ant world" to understand the mechanizations of Human society such as "conformity" and the servants and war and all of this kind of stuff.

And so—this concept that to "fully understand" would be a transference of *beingness*. And really, as we move up through the *Pathway*—and especially as you get into the Wizard levels of Systemology—we deal a lot more with the handling of mental imagery, the point-of-view of Self and its ability to direct that, but there are allusions to that within lower grade material.

And it's not that I'm holding back or anything; it's simply that this ability to access other points of *beingness*—this ability to get out of the confines of the Human Condition—simply becomes much simpler as an individual moves along the *Pathway of Self-Honesty*.

There is plenty of lore, whether it be the "shamanistic" concept of "shape-shifting" or the transference of the point-of-view into an animal form, or the idea of "communing" with nature spirits and the Dryads and the tree spirits and what not, by actually transferring or projecting—I mean, it's never "projected" from a point-of-view of being confined to the body: the Alpha-Spirit is never actually *projecting* anything any more than it already is in considering other points of view. It's not confined to the body; therefore there is no need to project it from the body.

However, many have already been confined or limited to this restricted consideration that they've agreed to—or kind of forgotten about anything else concerning the point-of-view. That this point-of-view is simply being adopted for *this* experience and that it isn't actually Self and it isn't actually who an individual actually is any more than an individual would *be* the "bear" or the "squirrel" or the "ant" simply by projecting it—it's simply a matter of consideration.

The individual is always the individual—the Self—no matter what kind of package or personality you want to push over that. And then, what we are doing systematically—when we deal with the multiple "Gates" or the "veils" or however you want to interpret that as you move up the "Ladder of Lights" or along the *Pathway to Self-Honesty* or the "gradients" of the various Master levels and Wizard levels—is we're peeling those layers back; we're not adding anything; we're not adding more layers to it.

Because we use these concentric models it seems like these other spheres and everything are being built up over it, but what we're actually doing is: each one that we're encountering, we're actually peeling back and freeing Self to be able to experience just a little bit more than what the previous "paradigm" or "level of restriction" is doing.

And so really, when you look at the backbone of the Druid

methodology, when you look at the Elven-Faerie nature traditions, when you look at the essence behind the Dragon Legacy and how its origins developed, it's really about looking beyond the Human Condition and even understanding more specifically how the Human condition was—we don't really use the term "conditioned," we use "programmed" and "imprinted"—the imprinting on them; the way the programs and systems were structured; the physical systems; the mental systems—and all of these systems contributing to a Human experience (which is, of course, being occupied by the Alpha Spirit).

As we move into deeper and deeper levels of the Nature mysteries, we'll look at more of the "tree lore" and "Nature Tech" that we can apply to this. Let us consider that these are simply "modes" rather than agreeing to how the Physical Universe *is* and what these conditions of the Human Condition (are)—that these are modes of liberating the point-of-view of Self *beyond* the Human Condition.

: LECTURE 22—OGHAM TECH :
(September 24, 2020)

One of the features of *Merlyn's Complete Book of Druidism*—as a Master Course edition for present purposes that was not present when we released previous editions of the past, like, as an anthology (*The Druid Compleat*)—this edition has the complete notebooks of my "*Pheryllt Researches*" and portions of the *Pheryllt Researches* were then spliced with excerpts that went along with those particular themes, when I composed "*The Book of Pheryllt: The Complete Druid Source Book*," that was published by Kima Global to go along with "*Deep-teachings of Merlyn*" and Douglas Monroe's "*Merlyn Trilogy*."[*]

So, what I did in this edition is I maintained the material that is in *Elvenomicon* presently still today as it's been for the last fifteen years, and then added as an appendix to the entire book, the "*Pheryllt Researches*." And so, if you're going to be dealing with Master-level Ogham Tech and forest magick and a "Druid School," this is some pretty critical stuff to incorporate.

Now, I've already—I've been asked, and so I expect in the next couple years—I've been asked to expand on my work on the "Elven Tradition" and "Druidry" and many elements of Grade-I. And so, I've decided couple with—to co-write with—Rowen Gardner; and Rowen Gardner has contributed some Forewords to, I believe, the *Druid's Handbook* and the *Draconomicon* in the past—and I've done some work with them in the past. So, I decided to go ahead and probably work with them on several aspects of expanding Grade-I material—for those that are using it, again, as an entry-point; and for those who are still coming into our tradition from those parameters.

---

[*] Now available in a collector's edition hardcover from JFI Publishing as *"Draconomicon Vol. 2: The Pheryllt Researches."*

So... *expect that* to be coming up here; but what I do want to do is present—a lot of the material is already present within the Master Course, it's just not set up that way. So, again, if you look through the material and the "Instructor's Manual" and look at the material of the *Pheryllt Researches* in addition to the *Elvenomicon* and the *Draconomicon*, *Druid's Handbook*, you'll see that this time around already, the "Route of Druidism and the Dragon Legacy" far exceeds anything we were presenting as "*The Druid Compleat*" in the past.

At a Grade-I understanding, you're gonna find a lot of material as you go into the "*Greenwood Grimoire*" of the *Elvenomicon*—or even the *Vampyre's Handbook*—you're going to see more of an emphasis on work with "Rays of Light," which is really just getting someone into the practice of handling "flows."

Handling "energy flows" directly is actually a very high level element of "Alpha" work—of Wizard work. It's practiced at Grade-I levels; seldom mastered. Because when we're dealing with "Rays of Light," when we're dealing with the "flows," the channels between individuals, the "conduits," a lot of this... and the way it's explained in the *Vampyre's Handbook*, it's all handling, basically, raw energy directly.

Now, we've found as an alternative to this, that handling "mental imagery"—or even the concepts of which these various "flows" and "energies" and response-mechanisms are attached—is actually a lot more effective; a lot easier. There's nothing wrong with handling the "energies" directly, it's just that at a Grade-I level, when an individual is usually just now getting used to the concept that they even exist, it's usually consider a higher-level work within even that grade, to start handling "Rays" and such directly.

The other element being: astral light—the concept of an "astral body." We know now at kind of a higher systemological level that these "astral bodies" are kind of "blanketing" this existence that we have here; they're basically bodies that have actually almost—not deteriorated—but they no longer have the same "power" and "function" and "solidity" to occupy as a point-of-view as, for example, what we're kind of stuck in *here.*

And that's why we're trying to liberate an individual *out of* the Human Condition while we we're doing all of this work. These "astral bodies" perhaps occupying a "mental plane"—"mental universes"—that once occupied with very... very much as a "beta-existence" within themselves, but for whatever reasons enough barriers, blocks, withholding—in terms of wanting to reach, and withdrawing *from*—and other elements were kind of forcing more and more condensed point-of-views of what we experience today.

So, "astral work"—"mental work"—*can* be employed; it's just that we have found at higher levels of practice that there are simply more effective ways (than what is demonstrated in conventional mysticism). I mention this because the concept of the "Astral Grove" is introduced within my writings—within the last fifteen years—mostly [*laughs*] ever since I kinda came to the realization that there was a way to get back to this other "Magical Universe" that we've all descended from; and one of the ways in which I thought practice of that could be involved, was getting back to the point where *Self* was able to experience...

There's a reason why those that are attached—or find an attachment to [*laughs*]—have any affinity with the "Druidic Paths," the "Elven Paths," the "Faerie Paths," things that involve "Nature," the "Shamanism," animals and so forth; there's a reason why there's an inclination there: because this restimulates a memory—probably several lifetimes worth of memory—involving this other Universe, this other existence, of which one did engage in a very fluid communication and perfect understanding with what was treated *there* as the "natural world."

There is a "mirror image" of it in *our*—on *our*—planet, although not nearly as vibrant until you're actually able to peel away some of these "levels" of (fragmentation) that kind of dim our sight of this world. But there's a connection there because it does "remind" us exactly of that; and that when we looked at, for example (yesterday), some of the traditions and Faerie traditions and Otherworld beliefs concerning this existence and whatever existence that these once physical and inhabiting "elves" and so forth—"Faerie Races"—that inhabited this physical existence and we able to be identified as such, were then moving *back* to the "Magical Universe" and taking up residence there.

Now, what we've later kind of discovered was that this Universe became kind of a lower-level consideration or "prison" or "penalty existence" of a lower-level Game than what was taking place up in the "Magical Universe"—or out in [*laughs*] the "Magical Universe," where at that level of existence, we had the original archetypes of what you see with the "Wizardry" and the "mysticism" and the "magic" and the "elements" and the icons and themes that are drawing someone into this tradition.

As one of the "Masters" or the "Instructors" involved with the Mardukite Academy, you would then be able to recognize these elements and work with them later on in "processing"—if you get into "Piloting" or other elements and the higher "Wizard levels." Because these are direct links and these are what's going to get individuals out of the confines of the Human Condition.

Many that are taking up these paths already have kind of an inkling that there *is* something more and that they're not strictly "Human" as *Self*. I mean, these are all things that many carry with them today. Just because they're not involved with *us*, doesn't mean they aren't aware of these things. But...*selective directed attention!* That's what we've emphasized in Systemology; and most individuals that aren't carrying a *full* realization of what's taking place, it's overshadowed by all the other elements of the material world.

Now, in terms of "Elven Tradition," "Celtic Faerie Tradition," "tree magic," "forest magick"—there are ceremonies for the "Consecration of a Newly Planted Tree," a "Rite for Planting a Single Guardian Tree" and "Dedications of a Grove" or "Stewardship of an Area" are all within the *Greenwood Grimoire*—what was originally called the *Greenwood Forest Grimoire*—(in the) *Elvenomicon*, which also appears in *Merlyn's Complete Book of Druidism*.

One of the reasons I had encouraged, at one point, more of the "Astral Grove" work was, of course, the "Elven Fellowship Circle of Magick" was meeting in Denver. Most of the work I was doing at the time on the *Elvenomicon*, back in 2004 even, was while I was living in Denver. Although there were a lot of parks and, of course, access to the mountains and Nature. I was writing, primarily at the time, for what was going to be considered an "urban" readership; and so the concept of using an "Astral Grove" or the concept of using "imaginative creative visualization" to operate "magick" was simply as an alternative to, you know, access to "natural terrain" or natural areas to operate.

So, if an individual wasn't able to physically actually go to a park or go to an area or have a "grove" to work from or maintain stewardship of or guardianship of, then using the "Astral Grove"—using visualization techniques—was an alternative. And this is something I still do impress as a very effective form of "magick" that virtually any of the results that can be achieved from actually working out a ritual area, drawing out a physical space, using physical tools, physical implements an all that—can actually be practiced *within* the "mental realm" because that's actually all you're trying to achieve anyways.

The *Self* is using the "body" and the fact it's kind of been restricted to this point-of-view of a "body" at still this point of

Grade-I, that is has to basically get the body—what we like to do in "objective processing" in Systemology—we're getting the "body" involved and the command of the body involved, and more command and control of the Mind-System that's doing that, by doing these dramatic outward "objective universe" practices.

If the same states can be achieved in the Mind without that —if an individual is able to achieve that—then all of this can actually be done at that level directly; in simply the operation of the Mind-System. Of course, this doesn't replace what we're trying to impress in terms of the "Natural Paths" and "Ogham Tech" and actually going out into Nature and engaging into these lessons directly, but again, this is one of the elements that's not necessarily relayed in the "ritual magick" texts or in what's considered "mainstream New Age mysticism"—that all of these are meant to be tools, meant to be assisting the individual, the Seeker, into achieving this greater control over the Mind-Body connection or control over the Mind-System or actually Actualizing Self as a Spiritual Being as the Alpha-Spirit.

That's what we're dealing with all the way up the *Pathway*. But like we've said before: sometimes a passive—or just a simple read-through—or basic demonstration or basic initiation, like, into what we consider a Grade-I understanding of the "New Age" or "Magick and Mysticism" is not a guarantee that an individual is going to surpass that an reach to new levels of realization, so long as they're simply fixed to this "magickal-correspondence-physical-universe" (type of) understanding.

But in terms of these assistive tools—so, within Ogham Tech, we have the Ogham Sticks: they're twenty sticks or twigs, same size, cut the same size, polished; I mentioned before you could use "wood chips" if you wanna make more "rune stone" styles. But these are specifically for divination and cryptomancy—and so each of them, you would have twenty, and each of them would have one of the standard

Ogham "fews" or characters; either carved into, or if possible, burned onto.

And then Ogham Wands are a completely different set of tools. These can range from six to eighteen inches. And if possible, what you want to do is construct them from the correlating trees. So, you wanna have a "hazel wand" that's taken from the "hazel tree" and so forth.

If you look into the *Elvenomicon*—in the back, where we deal a lot with the tree lore—you'll see that there's a lot of correspondences and other ways of connecting the attributes of the energies so that you can find substitute trees that could represent the same kind of energy pattern. And so each one of them, what you want to do is you have a long rod and then this kind of section up at the top that you have as like a handle, you kinda cut away this to shave it flat so that it kinda goes down into the middle and this kinda gives you this surface to either burn or paint one of the Ogham "fews" on.

The other part—traditionally what we do with these: these are used for specifically "tree communication" and "communing with Nature." So these wands we kinda sharpen the other point a bit, you know, cut it down to a point. And this is then put into the ground and so the individual, when their communing with a specific energy or their working on a specific "Path of Encounter" or what have you, they have this Wand into the ground and then they're holding the handle part here where the Ogham script is printed.

That's what these particular ones are for—and since their each used individually and their not "cast" as any kind of divination, you don't need to be too concerned with, you know, making them all the same size or anything of that nature; they're all—they can each just be individual tools.

And then there's another example of divination that you could use, which is just Ogham Rods. And these would be twenty-one pieces of the same size, like, dowels. You just cut dowels down into twenty-one little sticks that are all the same size, and you don't do anything to them. They're basically just "cast" out as, kind of like, the game of "*pick up sticks*"—they're just "cast" out and you try to "read" any... however they've fallen, you try to "read" any of the Ogham symbols or scripts or patterns in there that you might then look up to interpret as some sort of "omen."

Traditionally they've referred to the "magic pouch" that, like, an "Oghamancer" or a "forest wizard" or such would use, is the "Crane Bag"—because the crane is the animal of knowledge. When it would fly in the air and its legs and the way it would stand and different patterns it would make—they would interpret those as Ogham symbols as well. So they had these *bags* that were just called "Crane Bags." And so each of your sets, like your Ogham Sticks and Rods, they could each have a bag made to contain them.

The Wands, you can kind of arrange those. I've—when I've done this in the past, I had my own little wooden chest that I made; and I just kept all the various lengths of wood in there that way. So those are several tools that you can use; and you can correlate—you know, throughout this textbook there's all kinds of Ogham correspondences and correlations... ways of practicing divination or interpreting the Earth mysteries while using these. But that's basically the tools you might use for that.

And I should point out: although I don't really recommend this medium—the printed card medium for this—the original presentation of the reintroduction actually of this lore, the idea of a "Celtic Tree Oracle" really is attributed Liz and Colin Murray, which in 1988 released the "*Celtic Tree Oracle*" with St. Martin's Press. It's this beautiful green hardcover book and these cards. This has been basically the inspiration for much of the modern neopagan and "New Age" Celtic Tree lore and connected to the Ogham. This inspired a lot of interest in the Ogham, when prior to that, it was really more of an academic scholarly interest, concerning Ogham inscriptions that were found on stones all throughout Celtic Britain. There's actually even evidence that they're in the mainland of Europe, and even the Americas.

And so this interest in the "Celtic"... using the Ogham to represent a system of "Celtic Tree Magic" ended up kinda spurning off from that and later evolved into what's become almost an entire complete system and field of "magick." And there's many examples of, like, each tree listed in the back of the *Elvenomicon* or *Merlyn's Complete Book of Druidism*. The *Pheryllt Researches* also include many correspondences and applications and just a wealth of material that again, the herbal and forest tradition and so forth has almost become a paramount staple of the "general" magick tradition.

Now, one of the key tools also that I've kind of always popularized—I mean, I started this with the original *Sorcerer's Handbook*; it was given in the "Merlyn Stone" materials and also I've expanded in terms of the *Elvenomicon* and have further, I actually plan to take this (subject) further, as I said when I expand my publications concerning Route-D type materials (which will be coming out in the next couple of years).

So... the Elfstones. Now, this concept of "Elfstones"—they weren't necessarily referred to as "Elfstone" in ancient Celtic lore. What I did was—I was very fascinated with the "*Shannara*" series of Terry Brooks, and perhaps as one of this better known, it became the subject of the "Season One" presentation of it a few years back when they did actually make a televised version of it. We had been hoping for a motion picture of his book "*Elfstones of Shannara*" for decades—and it was finally picked up as essentially a miniseries.

The concept of the "Elfstones" is that there were these three stones which had significance as a powerful took; this set of stones. In that particular version, there were three blue stones. And I have a set that are three blue stones and what I use them for is "clarity of vision."

They were considered the "seeing stones" in one version of the stories by Terry Brooks, and so that's one way that I've used them. I've also used three green stones as a way of basically just being in touch with the "Green World" while working with some of the natural elements or the "Middle Ray"—the "crystalline ray"—things of that nature.

The traditional ones that appear, they're either known as "sky stones"—"triscale stones." They've been popularized in some of the old books of Celtic wisdom derived from mythologies; they've been found in—for example, the Pheryllt system presented in *21 Lessons of Merlyn*.

So, the traditional set is: a golden stone, a silver stone, and what would be a crystalline stone or a black stone. And these each represent: the "Golden Ray," the "Silver Ray" and the "Crystal Ray" of the "Druid's Cabala"; and the "Ray" system of the "Rays of Light" as they pertain to, not only the "Elven" system, but any of the "Light-Center" systems or "Chakra" systems or "Seven-Plus-One" systems that involve Lights, which we deal with all throughout the various grades.

And so these are actually a really good tool for getting in touch with basic divination and tree communication. They have kind of a "pendulum"-like "yes-no" quality to them; and so when they're used, the crystalline stone or black stone is used as an indicator. The silver is used to indicate "no" and the gold indicates "yes." And when you throw them down at the base of the Oracle Tree, whatever stone is closest to the indicator stone is, of course, your answer.

There's a lot of, you know, lore and mythology related to this. The traditional "set" consists of the Tiger's Eye for the golden stone, the Hematite for the silver stone and Obsidian for the black stone. And this, again, you can keep in a small pouch and keep separate; or if you want to make several steps the way I've... you know, a standard set that I've had since the 90's: the hematite, obsidian and tiger's eye. I also have a blue set and a green set and each I use for different purposes.

But these basic, just, focal tools—these basic implements... Again, it's not to put a lot of emphasis on the power that they themselves have, but over the significance that is attributed to it by using them—by using them as a focus or to concentrate on a particular "Ray" or particular state or particular aspect. And so for *that* purpose, they can be very useful; very useful tools.

So, before closing this out, I *do* want to give a brief rundown of the actual Ogham trees—and the most applicable way to do this, for the purpose of our Master Course, is to look at it from the perspective of "The 21 Paths of Encounter." As I said, you can look at them for their individual aspects—what they represent—each Ogham represents a color, it represents a bird, it represents a particular magical lesson—it does represent a tree. You can use all of these aspects in "ritual magic." You can use all of them for divinatory purposes.

But I thought, for the purposes of the Master Course, we'd give a run through of the "Druid's Cabala of the Forest" and how it's presented in climbing the "Great Tree of Life" from the Ogham tradition. The concept of "Ascending the Druid's Ladder" is interpreted from the Pheryllt tradition; and then this is actually put into the *Pheryllt Researches* portion of the Master Edition there.

So, it's not in the "Instructor's Manual," but it is in the Master Edition of "*Merlyn's Complete Book of Druidism*" in the *Pheryllt Researches*. And what this does is: this runs through the basic Ogham trees and the Ogham symbolism in the order in which it's given traditionally. And it's usually—they're in groups of five.

We start with the Birch Tree, which represents new beginnings, first realizations, self-sacrifice, change to a higher level, devotion to the Great Work, awakening on the path.

And then we move onto the Rowan Tree, the first action, the first move of a game, magical work begun, self-control, movement in the direction of your chosen path.

Then we go to the third path, Alder, which represents heated resistance, strength to face the avoided, conquering adversaries, the material world opposes your choice but your aspirations are completely protected.

The fourth path is Willow: new journeys and inspiration, Otherworld contact, confidence necessary, enchantment. Your path now appears as a dream on a moonlit night.

The fifth path: Ash; personal resolve, resolute decision, changing outlooks, the inner and outer world meet as one, and the inertia to break the threshold. And by threshold, we then approach the veil—the first veil of threshold—which is the "death of the old."

So, we've ascended up the path to the sixth now, to Hawthorn—where new blossoms awaken. This represents the first success or manifestation being purified, protection given as you accept the bitter and the sweet of the chosen Path. And the bitter and the sweet is interesting, because in the upper level, when we're talking about flows and we're talking about concepts in upper-level processing, we're actually talking about the "beauty" and the "ugliness," the light and the dark, the compelling versus the repulsion and all of that. This is something that actually as you break through the "Death of the Old," this is actually what we're trying to *flatten* out; *flatten* out any reactivity to.

The seventh path, the Oak: higher powers experienced and called to you, the strong door to the inner mysteries—remember Oak is said "*duir*" in Celtic languages. This is where we get the idea of *"Door"* and then, of course, the *"Oaken Door"* being considered one of the stronger common uses for the wood, as tradition extended. So personal reflection opens up to new possibilities; we're talking about opening up "doors" to inner mysteries.

Which then leads us to the eighth path, which is Holly. This represents an encounter, the Guardian of the Gates—which of course, we're approaching this Door; this Gateway—the self-worth is tested, balance of opposition, challenge is presented and things may not always what they seems so dispel all illusion.

And then we work into the Hazel. Hazel is the ninth path: the fruit of knowledge. As we know, the hazelnut—this kinda goes in with other traditions from Druidry—the hazelnut falls into the lake, which is then eaten by the salmon, and then bear eats the salmon. And these all become animals and trees and symbols of "knowledge"—of ancient knowledge and the paths of knowledge and ancient primordial wisdom. So, in hazel, the fruit of knowledge is given, wisdom is accessible, your encounter yields straightforward harvest of secret intuitions.

And then finally, the tenth path: Apple—Apple being the tree of beauty. So, we have this new enchantment; kind of the breaking through this first veil—the enchantment—such as like the *lunar level* with these new realizations and awakening these prior purposes and feeling the enhancement of Otherworld contact. This brings us then to the second veil or threshold, which is that "Matter Gives Way to Mystery." And so we're confronting "Mystery"—*flattening* "Mystery"—eliminating "Mystery" now.

And the eleventh path is the Vine, which is a meeting of companions, fellowship is born and hidden knowledge is revealed between them, strength to face destinies, your path is entangled with ... fate, prophecy of others.

The twelfth path: Ivy. And Ivy, of course, the "spiral"—the "spiral" of the Path, when you look at the growth patterns of Ivy; overcoming restrictions—Ivy, of course, breaking through barriers to be able to continue its growth—gaining confidence and inner strength and continuing to face the world; confront.

And the thirteenth path is Blackthorn: facing the material, the clutches of the world, transition and change along the path, death, loss, cleansing, clearing; when choices are taken away, the perfect path remains. And there you see another staple of the *Pathway to Self-Honesty*.

The fourteenth path: Reed. Experience in the world; learning from experience, understanding Earth systems, material struggle, survival, knowing selective conform...; knowing when to bend.

The Elder: self-annihilation; purging the Self of all artificial, the darkness before the dawn; the "Dark Night of the Soul"; facing truth, accepting lessons given and seeing clear light ahead.

Which brings us to the last set—the Third Veil—which is "Visions of Victory." And here we're coming down the "Home Path" here.

Begins with the Fir or Pine tree of high views, long sight, the depth of relationships; experience gives rise to new visions and new realizations; seeing past the illusions—and even past our own experiences—the distance... the distant clear path that is visible.

And the seventeenth path, Furze: the sweet smell of victory; awareness of the seeds born of difficulty; struggle passes away; and there's time to rest as you collect yourself. Here's where you're basically making that *point* where you're—it's either going to be a divide and conquer or conquest versus succumb.

And so at this point, you also have the eighteenth path: Heather. Pause and reflection; healing of the spirit; examination of actions—we're talking about overt (acts) and withholds; we're talking about the responsibility; we're talking about basically making one's Self "whole" so that one can aspire to the remainder of the journey.

Which, in the nineteenth path, which is Aspen: you have the rainbow of spiritual achievement appearing; protection given on the "Rainbow Path"—[*laughs*] you see many references here to the "horizons of many colors" and the "Rainbow Path." It's also—this is applicable to the Tower of Babel, in terms of the "Tower" of the Tarot; and so we're talking directly here of the "Ladder of Lights"—Ascent up the "Ladder of Lights" beyond what has been... breaking the gravity of the material existence.

And so the twentieth path, Yew, is: completion, final realizations, Ascension, rising above the impermanent, the product of the journey—the end is in the beginning; the beginning is in the end...

And finally, twenty-first path, Mistletoe, which in this tradition is representing the "formless," the "not," the "unknowable." But, in this essence, the "unknowable" is a good divinatory meaning for it—but in this instance, we're talking about the Infinite. And so we have the twenty-first element representing the "Infinity of Nothingness," which we know is, of course, the true background beyond the ALL.

: LECTURE 23—DRACONOMICON :
(September 24, 2020)

So, we've come full circle now, to the *Draconomicon*, because... I say that: it's kind of where all this began for me back in 1995. The *Draconomicon* started as, kind of, a smallish "booklet-pamphlet"-sized piece of material—and really evolved now to become what's this 25th Anniversary Collector Edition hardcover, which is the version that we've excerpted for the Master Edition of *Merlyn's Complete Book of Druidism*.

If anything, it was really a precursor to what later became the *Pheryllt Researches* or the "*Book of Pheryllt*"* recension that I did, or really even some of the work that ends up being carried on in the *Elvenomicon*, because keep in mind *Draconomicon* came first—this came before the *Sorcerer's Handbook* even; before any of it.

Really, this was my... it was only delivered very briefly. I only... there were very few copies made (and) circulated; really just (in) the underground in the mid-90's. And then it was incorporated bit by bit into the work of the "Elven Fellowship Circle of Magick" and other organizations I was working with and a few elements, of course, ending up into the product of the *Sorcerer's Handbook* released as "*Merlyn's Magick*" and then in "*Great Magickal Arcanum*."

So, it's been with us a very long time—as the "Dragon Legacy," it's kind of this undercurrent that's back behind the carrying of this tradition for, at minimum, now we're starting to go back prior to 2500 years ago; we're talking about thousands and thousands of years ago, you know, 2000 B.C. and such, and prior to that into prehistory.

---

* Available in hardcover from JFI Publishing as *"Draconomicon Vol.2: The Pheryllt Researches."*

The Dragon is one of those elements that appears with us directly in correlation with history; and so is a bridge—an iconic image or symbol—that extends from primordial—ancient primordial—history. And this is where a lot of history turns... crosses paths with mythology, because we're dealing with a time when there's considerably different presences on Earth—even if we consider that they were "humanoid," we know that prior to the types of "Human bodies" we see today, we know that there were a lot deeper distinctions; more visible distinctions between races, various cultures, various types of individuals, that were readily noticeable and which could be identified.

And then, of course, the identification of Self with those different personalities and identities along the way—and we see that with the figures presented in mythology; the Celestial Mythology.

We see figures that are very much spiritual avatars; they are obviously more actualized than the common individual was at that time, in terms of human populations. And they represent the "Celestial Mythologies"—the actual backbone pantheons behind all of these cultures.

Yet, when you look at the actual stories—the actual legends, the actual, kind of the, the themes behind the myths and representations of these various cultural mythologies, it's very clear that this is anything but an "absolute Divine" or an "absolute Holiness" or anything—that these figures themselves actually carry very specific program-parameters and identities and so forth that they were operating with.

And it's for those reasons that we see certain archetypes; we see, for example, the "Goddess of Venus," for example, representing—regardless of what "name" is given to it, regardless to how it appears or in whatever culture it appears—we see very similar themes attached to that and in the lore and mythology and legends that are accounted for that are attached to that.

That's something—if you're working from a higher "bird's eye" view and you've actually gotten through all the different mythologies and that's actually been something of interest to you, then this work can also be used to draw those parallels and to see that. That's one of the things that we do in Grade-II with Mesopotamia is: we're looking at the oldest representations of these archetypes, in terms of a Celestial Mythology, in terms of the pantheon of [quote; unquote] "Gods" that are appearing in systematizing these... the inception of civilizations. And you can very visibly see the pattern, which later unfolds with other cultures and other demonstrations of accounting for the mythology and so forth.

The original *Draconomicon*—which I later redistributed in 1996 with a little bit more than just my simply notes (my *Pheryllt* notes)—introduced my interest in the "Tiamat-and-Marduk" story regarding the "*Epic of Creation*"—the "*Enuma Elis*"—as it's treated in Babylonian mythology.

So that began in the mid-90's, because there's a concept of the "Body of the Dragon" is attached to all kinds of things: it was attached to the names given to the manuscripts that compose the "*Book of Pheryllt*" as the "*Body of the Dragon*"; it was also referred to as the "Earth," the Earth was considered the "Body of the Dragon."

And yet other than this concept from the "Pheryllt," I was not able to really find many elements of Celtic mythology that supported that ideal—most of them having to do with the "heroes" and the "mythology" and the later stories and legends and such, but nothing that focused specifically on this concept of the "Dragon" being the Earth.

And that is what kept pushing me back into Mesopotamia from the very beginning: is that *that* seemed to be a paramount aspect to, for example: in the presentation of "Tiamat" being this "Cosmic Dragon" and that it was slain by "Marduk" and divided in two—with the "head" being the

"Heavens" and the "body" being the "Earth" and the "Physical Universe" and that there was a "Gateway" kind of separating in between.

And this concept, although there seems to be allusions to it in Druidism, there was no piece of lore or anything that was being presented that actually formed the basis of that; it seemed as if it had came from nowhere. And of course any time this was given previously—I mean previous to my allocation of the Mesopotamia origins of Druidism—any time any of these "mysteries" would show up prior to that, when I'd be researching, it always seemed to point back to, like an "Atlantis" or some "mystery place" that we wouldn't necessarily be able to identify a source of.

But it's very clear that the Dragon became a very significant icon of not only the Druids themselves, but also the sovereignty that they represented. And this concept, in terms of priesthood classes and priest-kings and Dragon-Kings that carried a legacy from the prehistoric or more ancient times, we see this carry from the Ancient Near East...

A lot of various—not just in Europe—but we focus specifically on Europe, because in the European traditions, we see the development of not only Druidism, but the type of the explorations that have become very popular at a Grade-I level: these various revivals that have taken place in the last hundred, hundred and fifty, years, which are really a result of how the "Mystery Tradition" evolved in Europe.

Now, the *Draconomicon* is really a "holistic" approach to Druidism, because it does not exclusively use a Systemology that's specific to the "Celtic" tradition. I basically was working on the concept of the "Dragon" in total—and this evolved into many many editions before its current one, but it's not specific to just the representation of "Druidry" or "Druid Magic" in terms of the "Dragon."

It's also not a presentation of "Dragon Magick" in the traditional sense that you will find in other mainstream publications or such in the "New Age." Because what *those* end up tending to be is really the type of "ritual magick" and the examples that we've already given (over the past few days) that simply just plug in "dragon names" or "dragon terminology" or "dragon symbolism" *into* them in order to form a "Dragon Tradition."

That's why we've focused, in the Master Course, on the elements that are actually more universal, or which actually carry into other paradigms, because that's how these were actually constructed. And *it's not* very hard. I mean, any "Master Level" practitioner, by the end of this, working through all these materials and working through all this tech, would be able to essentially develop their own tradition—their own effectively workable "mystical magical" tradition; and even create a Celestial Pantheon for it and have all of it work very effectively so long as they attributes were always being met.

And so you can easily see—if you can do that—you can easily look back into each of these cultures; whether it's Norse or Greek or Egyptian or what have you; you can see how these basic themes were each represented and that *those* are the elements that make each of these traditions *effective.*

When I wanted to introduce the *Draconomicon* for the "Joshua Free Imprint"—everything was getting republished as Collector's Editions, being revised and being prepped for what was already being anticipated a couple years ago, which is the Mardukite Master Course, which of course, took us some time to get all these editions done. But, Rowen Gardner wanted to emphasize one of these key points, in regards that the *Draconomicon* was already dealing with controversial perspectives.

I mean, I was already tying in elements of Mesopotamia and such from the beginning, and while the concept being drawn from the "Dragon Priests" and such of Druidism as the "Pheryllt," and a lot of the inspiration was coming from my original initiation in the 90's with Douglas Monroe's practices—it wasn't a direct correlation of studies; I wasn't simply, as some were looking at from the outside, thinking that I was just some "Douglas Monroe clone" or something.

One of the specific differences that has always separated our two schools of thought—because his doesn't really pertain to anything regarding Mesopotamia—he runs a "Druid School" in that respect, exclusively from that perspective. But, there's been many points of controversy that *I've* taken on in *my* presentations of it, that Rowen Gardner wanted pointed out for this new edition—because it wasn't really as publicized before and that at this juncture we've basically reached a point where nothing's really being held back, so...

In preparation for all these materials, any notebooks or old editions or appendices... anything that had been taken out or removed or considered unnecessary given whatever reasons were along the years of the development of this work, was all kind of integrated back together, finally, before presenting these Master Editions.

One of the key points being: for example, this "Welsh Charm of Making." And it's ironic now—because I bring it up now that, they mention it in the "Foreword" of *Draconomicon*, but "*Ready: Player One*," the recent movie of that, employs, as a result of it's appearance in the 80's movie "*Excalibur*," the "Welsh Charm of Making."

This work that was done on the "Welsh Charm of Making"—it appears in the *21 Lessons of Merlyn* as well, and a lot of people never spent much time working with that other than just random applications of it, you know, we've known because of its presentation in "*Excalibur*" it involved invoking the Dragon's Breath and such.

And so, for the first time really, that was actually translated within our work—and Rowen Gardner was the individual that assisted with that back when I was establishing the *Arcanum*, actually. That started showing up in *Arcanum* and wasn't given much attention, and so Rowen Gardner decided to put it into the "Foreword"—and address it in the "Foreword"—of the *Draconomicon*.

So that the "Pheryllt Dragon Charm of Making" does actually mean something; it does have a translation. And it means: "Dragon's Breath; Spell of Life and Death; Thy Charm of Making." That's what's being said there.

It's been phonetically—the way it would sound—and so we had to spend some time really figuring out what words and derivations of ancient languages, because there's a lot of Celtic languages out there. And we had to come... spend some time really, figuring that out. And it turned out it was a combination of various things and was later reworked as Irish and such.

The other significant incantation or whatnot that you might find—it's actually found in the movie "*Dragonslayer*" and then is actually used also in the "Dragon Summoning" of Douglas Monroe's *21 Lessons of Merlyn*, is this Latin evocation charm. And you know, this evocation—it was used in those sources, but was never really given any attention outside of the neo-Pheryllt tradition of Douglas Monroe; and a lot of times has just been discounted.

I didn't have as much luck translating everything with that as we did with the "Charm of Making," because I haven't actually worked with anything on that. I had Rowen Gardner assist with the "Charm of Making" and then I did have some Latin translation notes concerning the "Evocation of the Dragon," which regards addressing the rock(y) cliffs, and that the mountain would give way and then inside was the Earth Dragon. And so, that's what it basically translates out to.

In the recommendations of "Dragon Magic" in Douglas

Monroe's work, he talks about stabbing the "Sword" into the ground during the recitation of this evocation, which of course it describing accessing a "Dragon" that is beneath the mountains and so forth. It's very similar—using the sword in that respect—very similar to... in the previous lecture regarding the Ogham Tech; use of the Wands being pressed into the ground... having a sharp point, putting them into the ground and holding the handle to complete a circuit. In his suggestion of the Sword: the Sword is meant to impressed into the ground and then not to be touched until the end of the ritual when it's removed.

Obviously, we can see that there is some significance behind the imagery that's being evoked in these incantations—which we have to assume, like, for example: if we're looking at it from a higher-level perspective, we have to assume that the power is not necessarily in the words or in the language—or that it's somehow, you know, the correct accent being applied is somehow triggering some change in space and time where... It's all about the individual; changing the "phase" or "point-of-view" of the individual in what's considered experience—the experience that they're having.

We see, particularly when it comes to the dragon, we find that mountains are pretty much the main—being that the Dragons are considered "Fire Elementals." Now, there are Earth Dragons, Fire Dragons, Air Drago... you know, and quasi-alchemical combinations of them all—the quintessence of them all. But in traditional allocations of the "Elemental Beings," we usually attribute "Dragons" to the "Fire Element."

And the other aspects of the "Fire Element" that we find—when we're looking at terrains—is the mountains; so we see a direct correlation there. And then of course, anywhere where they are called or represented: the pyramids and ziggurats, temples and burial mounds and whatnot, these are considered artificial mountains, and all of them being sacred to the Dragon or the representations of the "Dragon."

Even in ancient—the original Sumerian language, prior to Babylon—the original cuneiform tablets concern a dragon named KUR, K-U-R [*laughs*]. And so, this can be translated to literally mean "mountain" and so this idea of this—the Dragon and the Mountain being the same—begins right back at the beginning of literature (on) Sumerian cuneiform tablets.

So, the "same" in terms of the representation of the "King" being in command or in control *of* the Dragon. This had multiple implications as well, because we're talking about—in some of these motifs of, for example, the "Epic of Creation" concerning Marduk and the slaying of the Dragon Tiamat, we see in other examples, for example, there's "Enlil" and "Ninurta" and all these other figures in pre-Babylonian Sumer—are basically kinda forged into being a certain "role" of the Gods, by demonstrating that they had the ability to "slay the dragon."

And then of course, the idea there being that the Mountain and the Dragon and even the "artificial Mountains" and so forth—so the temple—these all being represented together and kinda blended and identified together in consciousness, so therefore the King was the one that was slaying the Mountain and also the "King of the Mountain" so to speak. Slaying the... having the command of it, dividing it.

There you even see the concept later of a "ruler"—of the King being the one that is able to divide and manage and calculate the land; his "rule," his "measurement" of the land and his decision of what is *within* the realm versus *without* the land *is* basically what is *true*, what is *real*, for the purposes of that Realm.

And so we see this in consciousness—the purpose of exploring this and the reason we study and its application to the *Pathway to Self-Honesty*—is that we can actually understand better, the associations that have been applied and imprinted upon Human consciousness over thousands and thousands years in terms of authoritarian dictatorship concerning orders of the systems that take place in Human civilization.

It goes from these "great deities" and "Celestial gods" that were also described as "Dragons"—that's just a term that is also used to describe them. And then, of course, it goes down further to where we have specific lineages of "Kings" and "Priest-Kings" and "Priest-Scribes" and "Priestesses"— all of which are of specific lineages that these "dragon deities" had a hand in manipulating; whether it be "genetically" or even just in their "instruction." These then become qualified, in the people's minds, as a representation of the same

And then as long as the symbols get passed farther and farther down, you could have people—just deputy guards now—being a representation of this higher force that's (impinging on), in terms of the experience of the Human Condition or Human civilization. It's all about a series of agreements and conditional agreements that... you can see, even as the descent of Universes or the consideration of further and further limitations of point-of-view and so forth; that an agreement—each one of these sets of agreements brings it farther and farther and more solid and expanding it and less of that original meaning—less of the truth behind it ends up holding true at the same time further along.

I mean, now you have people just standing on every corner that are considered representations or messengers or "intermediaries" between this authoritarian force and beyond. And so in that respect this idea—this "All Seeing Eye" idea— that the Gods see all, well, that simply just start to have more representation; more representatives keeping track of the ordered systems for them.

Now we get into the "*Enuma Elis*" or the "*Babylonian Epic of Creation*" a little more deeply in Grade-II and it actually forms the basis of "*The Tablets of Destiny*" in Grade-III along with some of the other "Arcane Tablets." But, for the purposes of getting through Grade-I, let's just focus on the highlights here that—if you're looking for references of lore concerning the Dragon as it pertains to Mesopotamia, you actually find four different places or different connotations in which the concept of the Dragon is used.

In one, you have Tiamat—which is basically the "Cosmic Dragon." This is the idea of the ALL being the "Dragon" and the idea that the Dragon—you've seen the symbol of like the serpent with its tail in its mouth, the ouroborus serpent; now you have the "Cosmic Dragon" represented with basically almost an immaterial "spiritual" concept.

But then again, further down, you end up finding that Tiamat gives birth to these other monsters, which are also "dragon-like." And so, they refer to some of these as "Dragons" and such—different various creatures that exist out there that were later commanded, controlled or conquered and sealed behind a "Gate." And this is a theme that you find prevalent [*laughs*] in all different kinds of facets of esoterica or even the fantasies that have been inspired by them.

So, then also "Marduk" as a member of the Anunnaki—in many respects, Marduk is treated, and the other members of the Anunnaki—are treated as "Star-Dragons." And also of "Dragon Descendents Of Tiamat"—this was inherently their distant... the Mother. And so this is kind of relayed in the tablets as well.

And then later, you see the "Sirrus" and other more biological forms of "Dragon" that are represented, for example, like I say: the "Sirrus" which is the Dragon on the Gates and Walls of Babylon that looks kind of like a *sauropod* dinosaur —you see that as well being given the classification of "Dragon."

Really these all became kind of associated as one and the same—again having a presence that represented the "royal" or "Divine" kingship or the "Divine Right" for example to

"Rule." All of this is carried down actually in the "Dragon Legacy."

And so this "Dragon Legacy" carries forth wherever you see this sovereignty being claimed: that the representation of the "Dragon" and "Dragonblood"—certain legacies of "Kings" and "Priest-lineages" and all of this—get carried forth for thousands of years as what is considered the representative of the "gods" or the representatives of the "Divine" for purposes of being intermediaries to the common people, and those that were dispensing and administrating the "Cosmic Ordering" as it relayed to the ordering of systems in (and) among the populations.

And so this transference of "Dragon" imagery is really the hidden backbone behind that—and it's something that's treated in little niches of the esoteric, and it pops up in various aspects of, for example, the "Masonic" and the different concepts of "Gnosticism" and, for example, the "hidden years" or "hidden legacy" of Jesus and different things like that.

You see this concept of the Dragon appear wherever this kind of claim to this is found. And that in and of itself—when we talk about, for example, the "Elven Holocaust" in the *Elvenomicon*, or the "demonization" of the "Dragon" in the *Draconomicon*, we're talking about the systems that play as, for example, the Church of Rome and the Vatican and such was rising; basically anything that represented the hold or the sovereignty or the true rights to demonstrate reign on planet Earth, anywhere where that was in question, they basically had to squash it, they basically had to demonize it—they tried to eradicate it however they could.

In doing so, they were able to install their own leaders, their own Kings and so forth. There was a time when the Kings of Europe and such had to be, you know, sanctioned by Rome and such. And so these same principles that were once applied, for example, to the, you know, we were talking about the Stone of Fal or Excalibur and such, where there was a representation of how "True Kings" were chosen or defined, we see this again now being passed on to the Church; which rather than being the representation of the Dragon, they basically turned it into the form of the "Devil" and therefore to keep people from considering it or looking at it, they made it a thing of evil, something that was dangerous, something that you had to be protected from.

And therein lies, again, this deep-seeded secret of basically changing the shape of what we understand as "Beta-Existence" in *this* "material universe" on this planet and experiencing it as Humans, where it was—the same elements, the true elements: all of the power and the mysticism and the systemology and the programming and imprinting—all of these elements that had been gathered and collected along the way and refined, were suddenly being used by, essentially, the Roman Church to completely re-systematize, and re-order and re-shape, the face of the Human Condition.

And they were, I would say, pretty successful in this endeavor. We are *still* in the shadows of it today—although there's many that just have up and blatantly sought to rebel against it. There's a lot of proc.... There's a lot of it that shows up in "processing" concerning individuals and their programming and religious connotations that actually can extend for multiple lifetimes; that have been carried along each step of the way.

Concerning "esoteric symbolism" of the Dragon: we mentioned the "Circle," we mentioned the "Ouroborus Serpent" —basically with no sides, with an unending shape, representing in essence, an Infinity, or rather a continuity; all three-hundred and sixty degrees, we see 360 as a significant number in ancient mathematics; and then also as a "Gateway."

We know that anything... that the Circle is a division of the Dragon and what once represented the ALL—and then any of these Circles, whether we're using a Standard Model or the Spheres of Existence or whatever, we're talking about divisions or fragmentation of an ALL—a wholeness—and each one of these "circles" on these models representing a division or a continuity within itself.

Another symbol that we see reappearing with the Dragon is the "Cross." The Cross being, of course, connected to ancient Mesopotamian symbolism representing the "stars," the "Divine," "Gods," "Heaven"—a symbol of the Cross that way: the "AN"-star... [*A-N, not "On-Star" as you might have in your vehicle.*]

And then, of course, the combination of the Cross and—or even the "T" or the *tau*—and the Circle, being of course the "Ankh." And then, really, the "Ankh" is actually the "serpent-coil" stretching around the Cross. So, you have it not only as an entrance of a Gateway point, but also as I say, it's actually represented by the entwined circuit of the—of what we interpret sometime as the "genetic" or "DNA" material—but this is considered another symbol of the dragon, as well as the "Spiral," this has also been connected to the "Spiral" and the "S" symbols; anything that is connected to the serpent—all are corresponding symbols that you'll find in "Dragon Magic."

Within the *Draconomicon* section, you're going to be running into, again, symbolism of the Dragon as it pertains to the lore of Druids, but to which the origins, we end up looking into Mesopotamia and the Ancient Near East to discover any real further deeper understanding of this representation; which it seems like in Druidry,

it's actually taken for granted already, so then, this would be the "bridge" to getting into Grade-II directly from the Dragon Tradition or Druidism, Pheryllt Druidism, and even the "Celtic Faerie" and other "Elven Ways."

: LECTURE 24—GRADE-I REVIEW :
(September 24, 2020)

[*Now, it is possible that in the course of only spending now three or four days covering this accelerated Mardukite Master Course that... It's entirely within the realm of possibility that in covering nearly 2,000 pages of information with only a handful of hours of lecture—that I may have oversimplified things; entirely within the realm of possibility there [laughs]. But I believe we've been able to give a really good survey of what the Grade-I "Route of Magick and Mysticism" and also the "Route of Druidism and the Dragon Tradition"... what they entail; how they can be applied.*]

One of the features of the Mardukite Master Course—the "Instructor's Manual" that you have and the appendices applied to all the Master Editions of these older materials that we were able to represent—is that they do contain a curriculum outline that follows along with the texts of the books as they were released, which was an outline that really I did after the fact in order to deliver quick presentations to go along with the books at the time—because this is not the first time that I've done any kind of lectures or presentations or workshops on these materials, but this is the first time we're doing it as a "Master Course."

So, one of the things that this one includes, which we've brought back, is—during 2009 and 2010, we had set up, I think, maybe it was until 2011, we had set up a "Forum"—a "Mardukite Forum"—that was specifically for the "Chamberlains." We had our website and our bookstore, but the purpose of the "Forum" was to have a social network that was exclusive to the "Mardukite Chamberlains" and the research organization at that time and the development of the material.

And so although for this Master Course we never really

presented a specific, like, "testing" system, where you would actually go through an review, with like a written test or so forth—but in the course of developing this Forum, we ended up establishing "Study Groups," which surrounded key questions that were raised. And these then became the "Review and Discussion" questions that were released in the original... it was a handbook for "Group Leaders" that came out in 2011. We've since discontinued it, because we knew we were going to be developing this stuff further now, but it was called "*Guardians of the Gates.*"

And this included "Discussion Questions" that could be applied to make sure that an individual was actually getting the gist of the materials—because at the time, everyone was doing a "Self-Study Course"; we didn't have nearly the type of membership numbers we do now and accessibility to support and mentorships and so forth, so it really depended on this Forum and individuals all participating and answering these "Review and Discussion Questions."

By the suggestion of David Zibert actually, which is one of our Mardukite administrators in Canada now; he actually was suggesting that we include this as part of the Master Course, given that we really otherwise have had no other specific, like, "Review Questions" or "Test Questions" to apply to it in the past.

If we work through these just to make sure—they are included in your "Instructor's Manual" there and they're included in the "Master Editions"—we might actually make sure that we've got a handle on this as sort of a graduation point of... [*before we take a "meal break" here and get into Grade-II later on*]—to make sure we've gone through all of this and covered all of this, since I have diverted wildly from the outline as it was prescribed, because I believe that at a Master Course level we can cover this ground pretty quickly; you have the materials there at your disposal to be able to review each of the facets a little more deeply—but at least now you've been able to see how they all go together.

Now, the first question: "How has the meaning of Druid, its organization and structure, changed since its inception thousand of years ago?" Well—I'm pretty sure we've been able to cover that in some of the lectures we have here, but just briefly: obviously we know that at its inception we had these various invasion points—the Elven races. We see the structure of Druidism develop as systematizers of the Celtic people as those populations continued to grow and civilization is kind of incepted there.

And then, of course, we see "de-evolution" of it, in terms of the rise of the Church—the rise of the Romans—and then, of course, its use throughout the Middle Ages and revivals and intellectual schools, underground societies and clubs; and then, of course, today, in "neopaganism."

How... now, question two: "How have the qualities and definitions of authority, mastery and power treated within the Druidic paradigm?" This is twofold: we, of course, know that as a material system or body, that the Druids were basically in charge of the structure of Celtic civilization; and so there is a certain amount authority, mastery and power considered—attached to the Councils, the material power of the Councils.

And then, of course, we've referred to the "magic"—any kind of "magical ability"—any kind of mystical experience—being basically subject to an individual's mastery and authority in those particular areas.

So, question three: "What classical sources of history and record-keeping have influenced perceptions of Druidism, and how?" We talked about the surviving records that kind of came out of the underground, in terms of the preservation of the Welsh manuscripts and the Irish manuscripts—the *Book of Invasions* and so forth—the mythology, but also its suppression and destruction with the Romans.

And then of course, the classical references: the Greeks and Romans being one of the primary ancient history sources that we have to allocate anything concerning the Druids.

The next question is: "Define the basic structure and parts of Elemental Ritualism, performing a functional demonstration." [*laughs*] Okay, we've talked about "Elemental Ritual Tech." We've talked about "Elemental Tech."

So, the next question: "How does an emphasis on connectivity and harmony with natural, Cosmos, Universe, &tc., affect Druid philosophy?" I'd say that's been pretty much covered as well. We've discussed—basically how it puts one in touch with the greater Cosmos; getting one outside strict considerations of the Human Condition, which of course, goes right down along with question six.

"What role do animal totems, ancestral honor and other forms of "shamanism" play in Druidic tradition?"—having to do with preservation of memory; the extension of whatever consideration of "points of beingness"; being able to redirect beingness—but also to separate those. To understand that the individual *is Self* at its highest point of Alpha... as an Alpha-Spirit. It's not the genetic body; it's not the genetic memory of the body. It has the ability to go *into* and *out of* the consideration of Beingness as other animals, but it is not fixed to one of those either.

And that we can observe and honor some kind of ancestral tradition—but that there's no reason for us to carry the, you know, "sins of the father"; there's no reason for us to carry along any deeper consideration of that, as far as the "phases," the "personality-persona-programming," anything that we might have inherited from those that we love or those that we've lost.

Finally: "What influences of the ancient Druidic tradition are still present in modern society?" ...oh, boy! Well, this could go anywhere from the most obvious, in terms of neopaganism, and you know, the actual revival of "Druidic Traditions" as such—to things such as, if we explore the seasonal aspects that are given throughout your textbooks there: different seasonal customs.

The idea of the evergreen being significant in winter, being that it remains alive so that the decoration of evergreens, the symbolism of mistletoe and holly. The practices of Halloween: the carving of pumpkins—of course, they carved gourds and fruit there—but the use of "heads"; the carving of "fruit-head-lanterns" to ignite—to light up—like a circle; a "ritual circle of heads" that were carved out of, what we would today use pumpkins, but they were using gourds and such.

Most of the common traditions—and this is why I say, even though you could study many civilizations, many different cultures—these European traditions that are left over from the Druids, are the ones that are not only common in Druidry and in European observations, but in your basic everyday customs today. Even the idea of the symbolism attached to "Easter" and the "Spring Rites" and "easter bunnies" and "egg hunting" and so forth—all of these various traditions have been handed down from the Druids and preserved in some respect in today's cultures. And that's not even to bring up the May Pole [*laughs*] and other such customs.

Now, when we look at the review questions for the "*Elvenomicon*" or "*The Book of Elven Faerie*"—the first one: How are the traditions connected to ancient Mesopotamia? And right there, you got the million-dollar question; because that's what's actually defined this as "Mardukite Tradition" or "Mardukite School of Thought" or " Mardukite Philosophy" as I set it down in 2008, versus every other perspective.

It's not that we are specifically and only—I mean, we do have "Mardukite Zuism," which is a "religious" Mesopotamian Neopagan, be it Babylonian oriented, revival tradition that emphasizes the use of the Mesopotamian tradition, or what we'll be getting into in Grade-II, as simply an alternative or further extension of this other knowledge. But—that ends up being really the subject base of the entire pursuit, the entire pursuit of Grade-I really, as it applies to Mardukite tradition, would be getting at its roots in ancient Mesopotamia. Really—that's a question that's essentially the wide-encompassing element of what we're doing; and can be discussed and described in various ways.

And then this just leads into the next question about how the beliefs of the more recent "fairy-faiths" of Europe are similar and/or different to the Ancient Near East traditions, Egyptian, Classical and so forth. And here again: you're actually noting a difference in the preservation of it as a rural folk tradition as opposed to, in the more ancient times, where these systems were set up as almost a "national religion" and it really emphasized being a citizen; being a part of the city-state; being a part of the tradition and customs as it was applied.

When you talk about the extensions into Europe and so forth, you have individual cultures and tribal developments taking place—and then, of course, this systematization of that with the Druidry. And then after the coming of the Romans and the Christian Church, the dissolution of Druidry and then, kind of, the recession of any kind of remnants that link back to these traditions in to the kind of rural, distant, and fragmented locations; individuals in their country cottages, living their own lives separate from the city and focusing on their relationship with the environment, Nature and what's going on around them, as opposed to city life, and usually passing that on in more—you see more direct apprenticeships taking place at that point, where someone is, like, passing on their knowledge and wisdom or tradition onto another during their lifetime and such; as opposed to widespread schools and colleges.

Then, of course: "What was the purpose of the preservation of Dragonblood and dynasties"—being, of course, the preservation of, like, a continuing line or descent representing that Divine Right to Rule handed down from a time when the Anunnaki were specifically—or whatever pantheon title is given to them—specifically designating this reign and rule and decrees and Order and Divine Will; and then choosing to these intermediaries to carry it on in their tradition.

And then, that leads us into question four: Describing the effects and purpose of the Elven Holocaust. Now, I didn't get into that too much for this Master Course, except to point out that there's a time period of history where, again, we're seeing the eradication of anything that stands in the way as competition for the Church to set up its in own power, control and sovereignty, and select its own system of government and leadership all throughout the lands which is was able to touch upon. And so, this is one of the reasons why I say, even though there is a time when this whole dynastic lineage traditional formation really did have some kind of significance.

As the influence of the Church took on more and more hold with that, you really see this kind of getting watered-down and so that's why I say, today there's really no benefit to emphasizing any, you know—regardless of what the genealogies might say or what a person's claims would be—we're just talking about "genetic vehicles" anyways; we're not talking about the operator; we're not talking about the Alpha Spirit—the I-AM—that's actually involved with it.

And so there were certain times when different entities did want to take on certain games and did take on certain roles and decide to play this out very systematically in this almost spiritual game of Divine Control. In today's world, what's really been seen to happen is that all of these elements—again, anything that's been found effective; all of the tools—anything that can be used or inverted or subverted for purposes of blatant material command and control of people and so forth, has basically been executed—been demonstrated—by these other more material worldly organizations with far less lofty goals, that have set themselves up as institutions of authority, all the way up to today's society.

This is why we study—why we are studying—this Systemology of not only the "Human Being" but the "Human Experience" that applies to even the systems that are at play, which have been put forth since ancient times, concerning the governing of Human Civilization, thought, emotion... just all of it—the whole imprinting of reactive control mechanisms being put in place thousands of years ago, and we track them along and see that those in control, those in power, those with authority, those demonstrating various levels of material success in this game, are those that know the rules of this game; they know how this all works and they know how to apply it all. Because they are very effective.

This is an *amoral* truth, okay? This is a very effective "Tech" going from, you know, all the way from the lowest levels to the highest levels—and that's all it is. It's an effective Tech; an effective "vehicle" or "tool." It's not concerned with morals and ethics—that all falls within the Observer and the participant and that which is operating this stuff.

And so those in control today have just the same effective ability to use these principles to, you know, bring people to lower points of Awareness and greater and greater enforcements of control onto them, as *you* would have in using the same knowledge, the same technology, the same abilities in countering that and even developing higher points of existence—higher realizations, working together with others to develop points—that are so far and beyond these that the policing of this low-level nonsense is just not even necessary.

Okay—[*laughs*]—this next one's actually asking about: "Define the seven aspects of Faerie lore." And I know I didn't really get into *this* [*laughs*] in this Master Course. But, they're listed as: the "Four Albans"—is number one, which is the annual ceremonial calender. The Druid Tradition uses the "Albans" as a calender; there's also other Celtic names given to them, such as "Samhain" [*sow'en*] and "Imbolc" and you know, "Yule" is actually a German term given to the Winter Solstice, but... Information concerning the seasonal rites and seasonal observations and customs and so forth is given in your materials.

The second basic is "Fairy Rings"—the idea of these natural growing circles, which is usually the result of different mycelium growth and such underneath the soil; but these different circles or patches that seem to set themselves off from the rest of the terrain. If you've seen a fairy circle in the grass or natural growth, you know what I'm referring to. There's a lot of lore and mythology and such attached to that about practicing rituals within one; if you were to fall asleep in one, you would be transported to the fairyland and so forth—different lore attached to that.

"Ley Lines"—they're discussed, or sometimes even referred to as "Dragon Lines" in the *Draconomicon*, but they're electromagnetic... obviously there's circuitry attached to the planet Earth as a system; different magnetic lines and currents and such that operate, given that it is *mass* operating within the physical existence of the *Beta Universe*, so it has its own circulatory systems of energies and patterns of that.

The idea of being "Elf-Shot"—the idea that there's these "games" and "battles" and different things taking place in the Elemental World; with the Seelie and Unseelie Court, and so forth—that an individual, a mortal, that would be accidentally hit by an "arrow" from one of these "Elven Archers" would be permitted a certain degree of "Faerie Sight," because they'd be able to see the individual, the Elf, that hit them, so to speak. And this appears in Faerie lore.

The game of "Foison"—[*laughs*]—this is a game where, apparently, we're talking about entities that have had an experience in the Physical Universe before, which have actually at one point descended here and then actually moved back out into this, kind of "Otherworld"—a plane, a spiritual plane, or "Magical Kingdom" so to speak—that there's a different level of solidity there. In terms of eating and foods and such, you see these games where the Elemental spirits or "fairies" or "elves" are actually coming and taking the essence of a food from it, without actually disturbing what the outside appearance of the food would look like.

I mean, [*laughs*] this is considered a "game" to them. But the same kind of concepts you've seen, for example, with leaving "milk and cookies" out for Santa Claus, which is supposed to be, like, this "Elf King" or so forth, originally. And so this was, you know, to invite and appease these helpful beings into one's life. And this is carried out in various "faerie traditions" thereafter.

One of the other concepts here listed as a basic is the "Co-Walker" or the "Just-Halver"—basically a "shadow entity" that basically follows along with an individual and is, kind of, leeching off of or absorbing, again, some of the essence or some of the sustenance that they take in and so forth. You know, this crosses with other lore: you've seen lore of the "Changelings" or the "Stolen Child" and all of this; all of this connected with these "faerie beings."

And then, finally, the "Sylvanus Folk"—which would be the "Wood Elves," the Woodland... We spoke before of the "High Courts" and the "Dragon Tradition" and so forth, and the "High-Born Elves" and these "nobles," but there is also the "Sylvanus," the "Woodland Elves"—the "Wood Elves"—and such; the "Nature Spirits" that are really just connected to the natural environment. They can be communicated and contacted with in the same.

So, these are just some of the aspects—well, it's called here the Seven Aspects of Faerie Lore. This isn't some like "Seven Pillars" thing; if someone doesn't know them as the "Seven Aspects..." I mean this isn't given as any doctrine anywhere. It's simply a list of basic faerie lore that just so happen to be seven parts and so it was listed like that.

The next question, dealing with the story of Reverend Robert Kirk, which we discussed. Basically, you know, finding out what an individual thinks about that, and how it could be explained in various examination of that case study. And then, let's see...

How is the existence of Man causing fractioning of the "Sidhe" ["*shee*"] between the "Seelie" and "Unseelie" courts similar to the division [*laughs*] of the Anunnaki lineages over the same debate? This is something discussed in the *Elvenomicon* and as a bridge to, again, working back to Mesopotamia. And we didn't talk about this too much, but what we do find is that in this transition period where we see the Elemental Beings, or we see these "higher beings" transitioning back into whatever existences that they go to *after* all these encounters with the rise of Human populations.

There is a "Seelie Court"—there is a sect that continues to remain in communication with the Human beings and assist them and which appear in a lot of this original "ritual magic" and traditions and so forth, with the faeries and the Druids and the Elven Way. And this creates kind of a schism in the organization in their civilization, because they're really not interested anymore with having anything to do with Humans because everything that's been taking place.

This same thing—this division—we find in the ancient cuneiform texts, if we're going to talk about anything in Grade-II in this respect, over the handling of Humanity after its attempted destruction of it, for example, during the "Deluge." And that Enki's decision to try to assist humanity through that period; make sure that it survived; make sure that the wisdom and materials and such could survive and be used to start things again—this actually creates kind of a schism, again, in the Anunnaki factions, in the fact that now you have Enki and Marduk and Nabu and the Babylonian deities differing from the traditional order that was set up under Enlil and the other lineage of Anunnaki.

I mean, eventually, they all end up being a part of Sumerian-Babylonian mythology and lore and religion; and they all end up setting up their own temples. But, there was a point when, again, the assistance of Humanity by these "higher beings"—the decision to do so—ends up creating essentially a schism or fractioning of the order of these particular organizations.

Now, when you're qualifying—if we're talking about the Mardukite Academy—I mean you might operate a particular Wizard School or classroom or particular course on any of these subjects a little differently; but when we're qualifying a Mardukite Master Course level of Grade-I material, we're really more concerned with the feeling and understanding that an individual has about all these things; we're not concerned with whether or not they can memorize a series of magical correspondences or whether or not they get through it and can remember that the seventh Ogham is the Oak Tree or something of that nature.

I mean this can be treated at an academic level that way if that's really the direction some want to go in. What we're really more concerned with—for the purposes of the Mardukite Master Course and for carrying a Seeker up the *Pathway of Self-Honesty*—is getting the general feeling of this material; getting a general feel of this Grade-I "Lunar Level" enchantments, mysticism, magick—and being able to realize that there *is* something behind this; that this stuff is exactly as its been put down as it has been developed over the last several thousand years—but that we are inevitably leading towards something that which is gone behind all of this and which has not really been explored very definitively in any of the materials or curriculum or what not that you're going to find, not necessarily here in the Master Course, but out there in the greater world-at-large.

This is a much different, higher caliber, presentation of a "Magic School," "Wizard School," "Magician School," "Witches Academy," "Druid School," "Elven Fellowship"—whatever you want to focus on at each level—than what you are going to find in the mainstream materials. You'll really find everything you need within here—especially if you're combining "*The Great Magickal Arcanum*" with "*Merlyn's Complete Book of Druidism*"—you've got the complete foundation of the entire Western Magical Tradition extending all the way back to Mesopotamia and including the Dragon Legacy.

In terms of my original presentation—the original design and development of the work along the way—we've basically gone through everything from 1995 up and through 2008, which really defined my own "Merlyn School," it defined everything I've delivered to you and contained with these two Master Editions ["*The Great Magickal Arcanum*" and "*Merlyn's Complete Book of Druidism*"]. Because essentially what, up until founding of Mardukite Ministries, I was delivering [materials] to my own apprentices and to Seekers at that time as the "Merlyn School."

So, this is really, like I say, a "graduation point." Because these two volumes present an entirely separate *Grade* from everything that's developed from that, when I decided to go even further back, back, back, and even up into Systemology. So, we've covered many points where they overlap—but they can really be explored as I say, a separate "school" and that in qualifying "certifications" and qualifying what you could deliver now, for example, if you were to leave here today—to leave the Academy today—and not continue on with the Mardukite Master Course, what I basically intended was that these lectures up to this point would be able to certify, for example, a "Level-One Instructor" in delivering purely the Grade-I type materials; that these lectures already given, coupled with the materials from *The Great Magickal Arcanum* and everything that composes *Merlyn's Complete Book of Druidism* that you would be entitled from this point on to, at the very least, be able to operate a "Magic School" or "Wizard School" or offer Mardukite Academy Courses specifically at the Grade-I level.

So, you can pat yourself on the back about that. You've been able to get through *half* of the Master Course [*laughs*] now, and been able to actually get to a point now where we can say that we've basically wrapped up Grade-I as I'm going to deliver and outline it. There's many other points and facets —many other key areas in there—some of which we end up tapping later into the Course, because again, they do overlap. But you could easily come up with many more "review questions"; coming up with unique courses that emphasize specific facets, and so forth, all the way through; and using these materials to do so.

And I do encourage that. So long as we've followed—you're using these materials here and you've heard these lectures, you've studied the materials, you're familiar with our presentation; you're fully empowered now to deliver the Grade-I material of the Mardukite Master Course.

[*So now, let's go ahead an we will take a lunch break and when we come back, we will be entering Grade-II material; be focusing on Mesopotamian Tradition, the Route of Mesopotamia, Mardukite Zuism proper and the Anunnaki, which will bridge us, again, into exploring the "Arcane Tablets" and the keys which have unlocked this amazing Pathway that we've discovered within our Systemology.*]

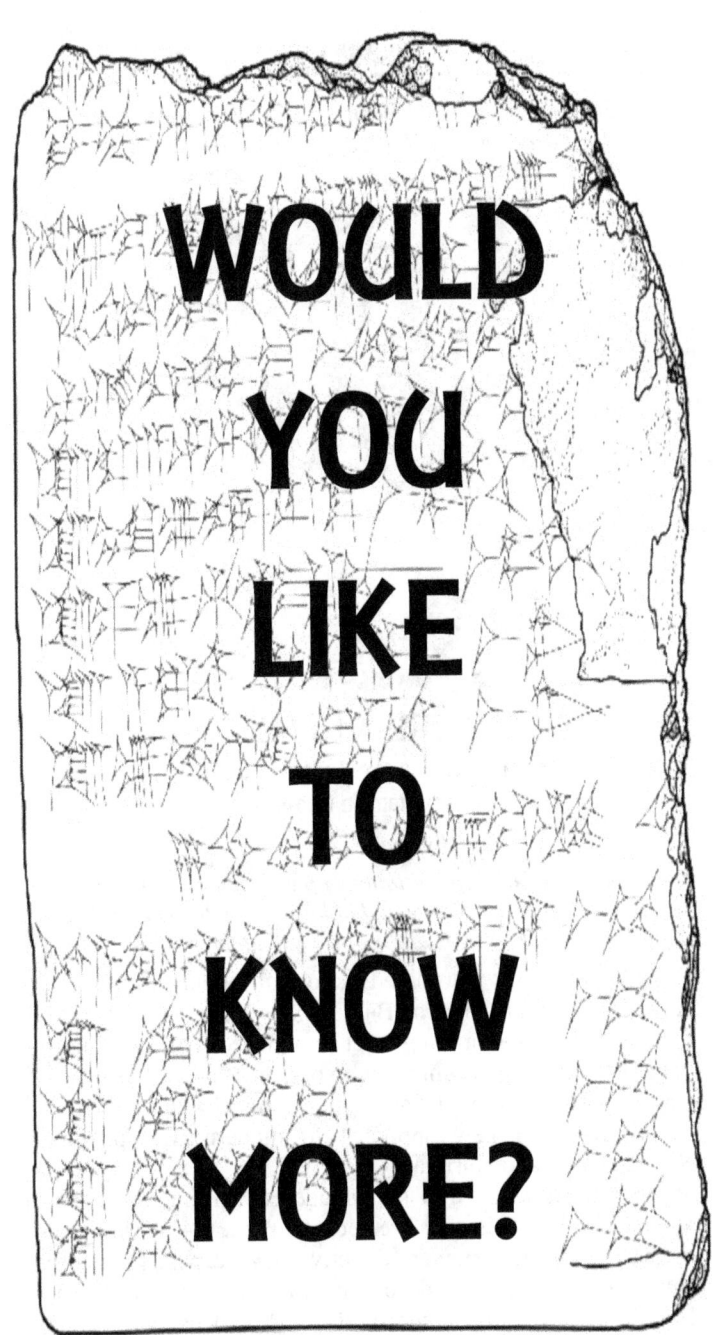

AVAILABLE FROM THE **JOSHUA FREE** PUBLISHING IMPRINT

The Original Classic Underground Bestseller Returns!
10th Anniversary Hardcover Collector's Edition.
Explore the original religion on Earth.

SUMERIAN RELIGION
Introducing the Anunnaki Gods of Mesopotamian Neopaganism

by Joshua Free

Develop a personal relationship with Anunnaki Gods
—the divine pantheon that launched a thousand
cultures and traditions throughout the world!

Even if you think you already know all about the Sumerian Anunnaki or Star-Gates of Babylon... * Here you will find a beautifully crafted journey that is unlike anything Humans have had the opportunity to experience for thousands of years... * Here you will find a truly remarkable tome demonstrating a fresh new approach to modern Mesopotamian Neopaganism and spirituality... * Here is a Master Key to the ancient mystic arts: true knowledge concerning the powers and entities that these arts are dedicated to... * A working relationship with these powers directly... * And wisdom to exist "alongside" the gods, ever to remain in the "favor" of Cosmic Law. The original precursor to *"Babylonian Myth & Magic."*

(*Mardukite Research, Grade-II Zuism, Liber-50*)

AVAILABLE FROM THE **JOSHUA FREE** PUBLISHING IMPRINT

THE COMPLETE BOOK OF MARDUK BY NABU

A Pocket Anunnaki Devotional Companion to Babylonian Rituals

edited by Joshua Free

10th Anniversary Collector's Edition Hardcover

Mardukite Liber-W Grade-II Zuism

THE MAQLU RITUAL BOOK

A Pocket Companion to Babylonian Exorcisms, Banishing Rites & Protective Spells

edited by Joshua Free

10th Anniversary Collector's Edition Hardcover

Mardukite Liber-M Grade-II Zuism

AVAILABLE FROM THE **JOSHUA FREE** PUBLISHING IMPRINT

SYSTEMOLOGY
The Pathway to Self-Honesty

A Concise Introduction to Mardukite Systemology

THE WAY INTO THE
FUTURE

A Handbook for the New Human

a collection of writings by
Joshua Free
as selected by James Thomas

now available as a Collector's Edition Hardcover

Here are the basic answers to what has held Humanity back from achieving its ultimate goals and unlocking the true power of the Spirit and highest state of Knowing and Being.

"*The Way Into The Future*" illuminates the *Pathway* leading to Planet Earth's true "metahuman" destiny. With *excerpts from* "*Tablets of Destiny,*" "*Crystal Clear,*" "*Systemology—Original Thesis*" and "*The Power of Zu.*" You can help shine clear light on anyone's pathway!

Carefully selected by Mardukite Publications Officer, James Thomas, this critical *collection of eighteen articles, lecture transcripts and reference chapters* by Joshua Free is sure to be not only a treasured part of your personal library, but also the perfect introduction for all friends, family and loved ones.

(*Basic Grade-III Introductory Pocket Anthology*)

AVAILABLE FROM THE **JOSHUA FREE** PUBLISHING IMPRINT

SYSTEMOLOGY
The Pathway to Self-Honesty
ORIGINAL UNDERGROUND INTRODUCTIONS
REVISED AND REISSUED IN HARDCOVER

SYSTEMOLOGY
The Original Thesis of Mardukite New Thuoght
by Joshua Free
(*Mardukite Systemology Liber-S-1X*)

The very first underground discourses released to the "New Thought" division of the Mardukite Research Organization privately over a decade ago and providing the inspiration for rapid futurist spiritual technology called "Mardukite Systemology."

THE POWER OF ZU
Applying Mardukite Zuism & Systemology to Everyday Life
by Joshua Free
Foreword by Reed Penn
(*Mardukite Systemology Liber-S-1Z*)

A unique introductory course on Mardukite Zuism & Systemology, including transcripts from a 3-day lecture series given by Joshua Free in December 2019 to launch the Mardukite Academy of Systemology & Founding Church of Mardukite Zuism just in time for the 2020's.

AVAILABLE FROM THE **JOSHUA FREE** PUBLISHING IMPRINT

*The Ultimate Necronomicon of the 21st Century!
Hardcover! Nearly 1000 Pages!*

NECRONOMICON:
THE COMPLETE ANUNNAKI LEGACY
(*Complete Grade-II Master Edition Anthology*)
collected works by Joshua Free

*And don't miss the newly released portable abridgment
of the original "Anunnaki Bible" scriptural edition...*

ANUNNAKI BIBLE

THE CUNEIFORM SCRIPTURES
NEW STANDARD ZUIST EDITION

Premiere Founders Edition for
Church of Mardukite Zuism

edited by Joshua Free

*Premiere Edition Hardcover
and
Pocket Paperback Available*

WOULD YOU LIKE TO KNOW MORE ???

It is time to take your first steps on the

SYSTEMOLOGY
Pathway to Self-Honesty

with the book that started it all!

Rediscover the original system of perfecting the Human Condition on a Pathway that leads to Infinity. Here is a way!—a map to chart spiritual potential and redefine the future of what it means to be human.

A landmark public debut of Grade-III Systemology and foundation stone for reaching higher and taking back control of your

DESTINY

(Mardukite Systemology Grade-III Research Volume, Liber-One)

AVAILABLE FROM THE **JOSHUA FREE** PUBLISHING IMPRINT

SYSTEMOLOGY
The Pathway to Self-Honesty

CRYSTAL CLEAR

(Handbook for Seekers)

Self-Actualization and Spiritual Ascension in This Lifetime

by Joshua Free

Mardukite Systemology Grade-III, Liber-2B

Revised Edition

available exclusively as an Academy Collector's Hardcover Edition

Take control of your destiny and chart the first steps toward your own metahuman spiritual evolution. Realize new potentials of the Human Condition with a Self-guiding handbook for Self-Processing toward Self-Actualization in Self-Honesty using actual techniques and training provided for the original "Mardukite Self-Defragmentation Course Program" —once only available directly and privately from the underground International Systemology Society.

Discover the amazing power behind the applied spiritual technology used for counseling and advisement in the Mardukite Zuism tradition.

(Revised Second Edition Now Available!)

AVAILABLE FROM THE **JOSHUA FREE** PUBLISHING IMPRINT

SYSTEMOLOGY
The Pathway to Self-Honesty

SYSTEMOLOGY HANDBOOK

The ultimate operator's manual to the Human Condition and unlocking the true power of the Spirit.

** *"Modern Mardukite Zuism"* **
** *"The Tablets of Destiny"* **
** *"Crystal Clear"* **
** *"The Power of ZU"* **
** *"Systemology—Original Thesis"* **
** *Human, More Than Human* **
** *Defragmentation* **
** *Patterns & Cycles* **
** *Transhuman Generations* **

(Complete Grade-III Master Edition Anthology)

AVAILABLE FROM THE **JOSHUA FREE** PUBLISHING IMPRINT

MARDUKITE MASTER COURSE
Keys to the Gates of Higher Understanding

Now you can experience the Legendary "Master Course" from anywhere in the Universe, exactly as given in person by Joshua Free to the "Mardukite Academy of Systemology" in September 2020.

800+ pages of materials collected in this volume provide Seekers with full transcripts to all *48 Academy Lectures* of the legendary *"Mardukite Master Course"* combined with all course outlines, supplements and critical handouts from the original *"Instructor's Manual"*—making this the most complete definitive single-source delivery of New Age understanding and spiritual technology.

Referencing 25 years of research, development and publishing, including *"Necronomicon: The Complete Anunnaki Legacy," "The Great Magickal Arcanum," "The Systemology Handbook"* and *"Merlyn's Complete Book of Druidism."*

AVAILABLE FROM THE **JOSHUA FREE** PUBLISHING IMPRINT

SYSTEMOLOGY
The Gateways to Infinity

METAHUMAN DESTINATIONS

Piloting the Course to Homo Novus

Written by Joshua Free
Foreword by David Zibert

Mardukite Systemology Grade-IV Metahumanism Professional Pilot Course, Liber-Two*

exclusively available in a hardcover premiere first edition

Drawing from the "Arcane Tablets" and nearly a year of additional research, experimentation and workshops since the introduction of applied spiritual technology and systematic processing methods, Joshua Free provides the ground-breaking manual for those seeking to correct—or "defragment"—the conditions that have trapped viewpoints of the Spirit into programming and encoding of the Human Condition.

Experience the revolutionary professional course in advanced spiritual technology for Mardukite Systemologists to "Pilot" the way to higher ideals that can free us from the Human Condition and return ultimate command and control of creation to the Spirit.

(*Includes Grade-IV Liber-2C, Liber-2D and Liber-3C)

AVAILABLE FROM THE **JOSHUA FREE** PUBLISHING IMPRINT

SYSTEMOLOGY
The Gateways to Infinity

IMAGINOMICON

Accessing the Gateway to Higher Universes

A New Grimoire for the Human Spirit

by Joshua Free

Mardukite Systemology Grade-IV Metahumanism, Wizard Level-0, Liber-3D

available in both as premiere hardcover or revised collector's edition

The Way Out. Hidden for 6,000 Years.
But now we've found the Key.
A grimore to summon and invoke, command and control,
the most powerful spirit to ever exist.
Your Self.

Access beyond physical existence.
Fly free across all Gateways.
Go back to where it all began and reclaim that
personal universe which the *Spirit* once called "*Home*."

Break free from the Matrix;
command the Mind and control the Body
from outside those systems
— because *You* were never "human" —
fully realize what it means to be a *spiritual being*,
then rise up through the Gateways to Higher Universes
and *BE*.

AVAILABLE FROM THE **JOSHUA FREE** PUBLISHING IMPRINT

*Original underground classics.
Joshua Free's bestselling
"Druid Trilogy"*

DRACONOMICON
The Book of Ancient Dragon Magick
25th Anniversary Hardcover
Collector's Edition
by Joshua Free

THE DRUID'S HANDBOOK
Ancient Magick for a New Age
20th Anniversary Hardcover
Collector's Edition
by Joshua Free

ELVENOMICON -or- SECRET TRADITIONS OF ELVES AND FAERIES
The Book of Elven Magick
& Druid Lore
15th Anniversary Hardcover
Collector's Edition
by Joshua Free

*All three Grade-I Route-D titles
(...plus additional material...)
now available in the anthology:*

**Merlyn's Complete
Book of Druidism**
by Joshua Free.

AVAILABLE FROM THE **JOSHUA FREE** PUBLISHING IMPRINT

SYSTEMOLOGY
Gateways to Infinite Self-Honesty

THE WAY OF THE WIZARD
(Utilitarian Systemology)
A New Metahuman Ethic
by Joshua Free

The Systemology Society Beta-Defragmentation Booster
and stabilizer for upper-level Wizard Grades.
Based on the "Freedom From" Grade-IV lecture series
given by Joshua Free in July 2021 at Mardukite Academy
and developmental research for the remaining year.

Accumulated involvement in dangerous situations, states of
confusion, unjust destruction and being at the effect end of faulty
—or blatantly false—information, all lend to fragmented purposes
that are non-survival (or counter-survival) oriented, leading us
away from routes to achieve "greater heights"—higher more ideal
states of Knowing and Beingness—including the
"Magic Universe" preceding this one.

(*Mardukite Systemology Grade-IV-V Bridge, Liber-Three/3E*)

THE MARDUKITE RESEARCH LIBRARY ARCHIVE COLLECTION

AVAILABLE FROM THE **JOSHUA FREE** PUBLISHING IMPRINT

Necronomicon: The Anunnaki Bible : 10th Anniversary Collector's
   Edition—LIBER-N,L,G,9+W-M+S (*Hardcover*)

*Gates of the Necronomicon : The Secret Anunnaki Tradition of
   Babylon :* 10th Anniversary Collector's Edition—
   LIBER-50,51/52,R+555 (*Hardcover*)

*Necronomicon—The Anunnaki Grimoire : A Manual of Practical
   Babylonian Magick :* 10th Anniversary Collector's Edition—
   LIBER-E,W/Z,M+K (*Hardcover*)

The Complete Anunnaki Bible: A Source Book of Esoteric Archaeology
   —LIBER-N,L,G,9+W-M+S (*Hardcover and Paperback*)

*Anunnaki Bible : The Cuneiform Scriptures—New Standard
   Zuist Edition :* Abridged Pocket Version (*Hardcover & Paperback*)

*Sumerian Religion : Introducing the Anunnaki Gods of Mesopotamian
   Neopaganism :* 10th Anniv. Collector's Ed.—LIBER-50 (*Hardcover*)

*Babylonian Myth & Magic : Anunnaki Mysticism of Mesopotamian
   Neopaganism :* 10th Anniv. Coll. Ed.—LIBER-51+E (*Hardcover*)

*The Complete Book of Marduk by Nabu : A Pocket Anunnaki
   Devotional Companion to Babylonian Prayers & Rituals :*
   10th Anniversary Collector's Edition—LIBER-W+Z (*Hardcover*)

*The Maqlu Ritual Book : A Pocket Companion to Babylonian
   Exorcisms, Banishing Rites & Protective Spells :*
   10th Anniversary Collector's Edition—LIBER-M (*Hardcover*)

*Novem Portis: Necronomicon Revelations & Nine Gates of the Kingdom
   of Shadows :* 10th Anniv. Collector's Ed.—LIBER-R+9 (*Hardcover*)

*Elvenomicon—or—Secret Traditions of Elves & Faeries : Elven Magick
   & Druid Lore :* 15th Anniv. Collector's Ed.—LIBER-D (*Hardcover*)

Draconomicon : The Book of Ancient Dragon Magick
   25th Anniversary Collector's Edition—LIBER-D3 (*Hardcover*)

The Druid's Handbook : Ancient Magick for a New Age
   20th Anniversary Collector's Edition—LIBER-D2 (*Hardcover*)

The Sorcerer's Handbook : A Complete Guide to Practical Magick
   21st Anniversary Collector's Edition—(*Hardcover*)

The Witch's Handbook : A Complete Grimoire of Witchcraft
   21st Anniversary Collector's Edition—(*Hardcover*)

The Vampyre's Handbook : Secret Rites of Modern Vampires
   5th Anniversary Collector's Edition—LIBER V1+V2 (*Hardcover*)

∞

19 95   20 20
JOSHUA FREE

PUBLISHED BY THE **JOSHUA FREE** IMPRINT REPRESENTING
**The Founding Church of Mardukite Zuism
& Mardukite Academy of Systemology**

mardukite.com

www.ingramcontent.com/pod-product-compliance
Lightning Source LLC
Chambersburg PA
CBHW050331010526
44119CB00004B/117